What Others Have To Say

During his 15 years of public service in Washington, Terry Lynch worked to improve the lives of American school children and people with disabilities. This superb book enhances all our lives.

> Gene Eidenberg, Assistant to the President and Secretary to the Cabinet, Administration of President Jimmy Carter, 1978—1981

Terry Lynch shares his caregiving experiences in a wonderful, thoughtful and down-to-earth guide to helping elders maintain their independence and dignity.

> Ken Dychtwald, Ph.D., CEO of Age Wave and Author of *Age Wave, Healthy Aging* and *The Power Years*

If this unique guide had been available during my time at Yale, it would no doubt have become one of our Worklife program's most vital resources for caregiving employees.

> Peter D. Vallone, Associate Vice President for Administration, Yale University (Retired)

Terry Lynch helped me find the courage to resist extraordinary pressure from the healthcare system to place my father in a nursing home after his stroke. Then Terry helped me with a homecare plan that lead to a recovery by my dad that was nothing short of astonishing.

> Cory Jacobson, Owner, Phoenix Theatres, Detroit, Michigan

One of Terry Lynch's chapters is "Making Things Happen." It could just as well have been the title of this incomparable book.

> Anthony J. (Toby) Moffett, Chariman, PLM Group, Washington D.C.

Life does not have to end at the nursing home door and Terry Lynch illustrates how families and staff can ensure that it doesn't. Every administrator committed to fostering a "person-centered" nursing home culture must read this book.

Erik Scribner, St. Paul Elder Services, Inc.,
Kaukauna, Wisconsin

Terry Lynch shows us that eldercare services are not only about coping with increasing dependency — he guides us to solutions that preserve and restore the independence of older people, and their families' peace of mind.

Karen Musser, CEO, Care Wisconsin First,
Madison, Wisconsin

"But I Don't *Want* Eldercare!"

Helping Your Parents Stay As Strong As They Can As Long As They Can

Terry Lynch

"But I Don't *Want* Eldercare!"
Helping Your Parents Stay As Strong As They Can As Long As They Can
By Terry Lynch

Copyright © 2008 Terry Lynch
Published by
The Legal Center for People with Disabilities and Older People
455 Sherman Street, Suite 130
Denver, Colorado 80203

This publication is designed to provide accurate and authoritative information with regard to the subject matter covered. It is sold with the understanding that the publisher and the author are not engaged in rendering legal, accounting, or other professional advice. If legal advice or other expert assistance is required, the services of a competent professional person should be sought.

First Edition

Publisher's Cataloging-In-Publication Data
(Prepared by The Donohue Group, Inc.)

Lynch, Terry (Terry Philip), 1938-
   "But I don't want elder care!" : helping your parents stay as strong as they can as long as they can / Terry Lynch. -- 1st ed.

   p. ; cm.

   Includes index.
   ISBN: 978-0-9770179-6-6

1. Aging parents--Care--Handbooks, manuals, etc. 2. Older people--Care--Handbooks, manuals, etc. 3. Caregivers--Handbooks, manuals, etc. I. Title.

HQ1063.6 .L963 2008
306.874084/6   2008927539

Cover and Book Design by MacGraphics Services
Edited by Terry Folkedahl Backmann (Wisconsin) and
Joyce Miller, Integrated Writer Services
Production coordinated by Mary Anne Harvey and Julie Z. Busby, The Legal Center
Indexing by Katie Banks, Eagle-Eye Indexing
Printing by United Graphics, Inc.

Table of Contents

Foreword

I first met Terry Lynch in 1981 when he was the program officer for a newly created national protection and advocacy system for people with developmental disabilities funded by the U.S. Department of Health and Human Services in Washington, DC. He was insightful, energetic, and extraordinarily helpful in advancing the mission of these programs, and he became the standard against which I evaluated the assistance of other government program staff.

When Terry left Washington to return to Racine, Wisconsin, in 1985, we maintained our friendship, and I had the privilege of meeting his mother Leila who was the inspiration for this book.

I also had the opportunity to hear Terry's presentation on caring for aging parents at a conference. I carried the concept of Terry's "campaign for Leila" with me over the years, and it served me well in the final chapters of my own parents' lives not so long ago.

I was delighted to learn that Terry intended to share his experience and his advice in a book. After reviewing Terry's manuscript and deliberating with my colleague Randy Chapman, we recommended to our Board of Directors that The Legal Center publish this book. They enthusiastically agreed.

The Legal Center's history is about people living in the community—either moving people out of institutions and nursing homes—or keeping them from going into these places. In our formal role as Colorado's Protection and Advocacy System, and as the administrator of Colorado's State Long-Term Care Ombudsman Program, we have embraced the values of empowerment, self-determination, independence and inclusion. We understand firsthand what happens to people who are denied these opportunities.

Terry Lynch's book is an important consumer empowerment resource. It is easy to understand, and it is inspiring. We have only to look at the current state of long-term care and the approaching wave of baby boomers to understand how important it is to change how we care for our parents and ourselves in the future. People who are able to stay in their own homes are healthier and happier.

We have a major obligation to educate people about their rights, and we also believe that this information should be accessible and understandable. Neither the law nor human services systems are necessarily consumer friendly. We must provide information to help people understand the law and make their way through the human services and health care mazes they encounter.

Diverting older people from nursing homes after a hospitalization is truly an option, and Terry's book gives life to that possibility. Nursing home care is the most expensive option for individuals or their families, and the publicly funded system often provides inferior care. By helping people remain as independent as possible and supporting them in home or home-like environments, we are able to see better outcomes and better quality of life.

We are proud to bring this publication to life and share this message with all of you.

Mary Anne Harvey
Executive Director

The Legal Center for People
with Disabilities and Older People
Publisher

Author's Note

Late in 2006 I asked Mary Anne Harvey, Executive Director of The Legal Center, to comment on the manuscript for this book. Mary Anne called to say they had suggestions for improving the book, but, beyond that, "How would you feel about us publishing it?" After collapsing in my chair, I replied, in my most professional manner: "Are you serious!?"

In May of 2007 I flew to Denver to meet with Mary Anne and Randy Chapman, The Legal Center's Director of Legal Services. We had worked together years before, across many miles, on behalf of people with disabilities. Twenty-two years later, The Legal Center was a force within the powerful National Disability Rights Network and I was allied with them in another important mission: promoting the best interests of older people and their families.

Randy Chapman is a prominent legal advocate and author with little spare time. At lunch in his favorite Denver diner he told me he had read my manuscript twice to be sure they should publish it. Then he asked what had motivated me to undertake the most demanding project of my professional life. I told him I could summarize it in three sentences:

▶ "It shouldn't have happened to my mother, to me, or to many others I have met along the way."

▶ "It doesn't *have* to happen."

▶ "I have to let people know!"

I am honored that Mary Anne, Randy, the Board and staff of The Legal Center have committed their time, talents and resources to this cause.

Without their help...

This book is much better than it would have been without friends who had little time to help but did so anyway. They include experts in healthcare, homecare, aging and social services, disability rights, financial and estate planning and residential services. The insightful comments of older people and of adult children concerned about their parents have been invaluable.

Many thanks to Therese Ahlers, Suzanne Barney, Suzy Breedlove, Heather Bruemmer, Bill Chandek, Maureen Eisenman, Sandy Engel, Ninna Frank, Bryna Fraser, Sonya Gottfredsen-Kromke, Mary Hanneman, Laura Hanson, Chris Hendrickson, Wendy Holt, Joan Karan, Marilyn Joyce, Todd Krewal, Hunter Moorman, Dave Paulson, Jean Rumachik, Nancy Schutz, Greg Schutz, Barb Tylenda, Robin Wilson and John Wray. You educated and energized me.

Lynn Breedlove, Marcie Brost, Dennis Harkins, Tom Hlavacek and John O'Brien guided me into the Wisconsin world of grassroots advocacy and enriched my understanding of the restorative powers of family, friends and community. And it's about time I told Roy Froemming, Terri Johnson, Pat Kelly, Mark Sweet and Susan Tess how much they taught me.

Lynn Breedlove has been a constant ally throughout the development of this book. Dick Joyce gave many productive hours between matches during two golf vacations. Anna Chavez has been extraordinarily generous with her time and talents.

Sandra Christensen got me through writer's block, inspired and encouraged me along the way and never said "not now" in response to my "please help me figure this out" calls. Terry Folkedahl Backmann brought to this project her enthusiasm, her formidable editing skills, and made me a better writer. Denise Krewal devoted hours of skilled and painstaking work to the Resource Appendix. Jana McLaughlin, a colleague and skilled professional photographer, literally donated her time and expertise to restoring the photographs for this book.

Any writer whose book and cover designer is not only talented and creative but also committed to his cause is more than fortunate. Kerrie Lian: Thanks for everything!

And then there is Wilsons' Coffee and Tea. I can't imagine a better office or community meeting place. Without your hospitality, friendship, support—and coffee — I would probably still be on Chapter 3.

To Leila Lynch

My lifelong teacher
and
My lifelong friend

Introduction

How Did I Learn What I Know?

In 1985 I left my federal government job in Washington, D.C. and moved back to Wisconsin to start an independent-living consulting business. I specialize in helping older people and people with disabilities remain as self–reliant and involved in community life as possible. Soon after starting my business I was living my work. It was then that my real education in "independent living" began.

Until her mid-70s, my mother, Leila Lynch, had been vigorously involved in life in Wisconsin, with an interlude in Colorado. I will refer to her as "Leila" (pronounced Lee-I-Lah). Leila was raised in western Wisconsin and was known as "a high-spirited girl" who rode ponies bareback on the Erickson family farm. She moved to Racine, Wisconsin at 21 to teach elementary school. Leila met and married my father, Gerry Lynch. On a whim, they moved to Denver, where I was born. I had a year to enjoy the Rocky Mountains before Gerry and Leila decided to return to Racine. Leila stayed home to raise me.

When I began high school she returned to teaching. Then she moved on to a contented and active retirement with my dad. After he passed away,

Leila adjusted as well as one can and went on with life. In her late 70s, Leila's strength and vitality began to erode. She had several injuries from falls. During my last two years in Washington, she spent her winters with me.

When I returned to Wisconsin, Leila and I became housemates in our family home in Racine, a small city on Lake Michigan between Milwaukee and Chicago. Leila remained somewhat self-reliant while we were in Washington, but shortly after we moved back to Racine more injuries and a rapid decline in memory stole her ability to manage everyday life. I was no longer just a son. I also was my mother's caregiver.

Although Leila required constant care after that, she continued to find pleasure in life. She remained at home until her death in 1995 at 89. Relatively unique circumstances enabled me to provide Leila the help she needed: She and I were good friends, I could run my business from home, and we benefited from government programs that enabled me to employ in-home workers for several hours each day, often more. Leila had to spend most of her savings before she qualified for this government aid.

During those years with Leila, I

▶ worked with her physicians to find effective treatments for her medical problems;

▶ helped her survive a series of medical crises;

▶ developed a supportive network of neighbors, volunteers and in-home caregivers; and

▶ tapped into a variety of helpful community services.

Ultimately, I also was able to manage my overloaded life.

This is the guide I wish I'd had before Leila's health problems changed both of our lives. It sums up what I learned in those years and in my work with other adult children, whose relationships with their parents sometimes have been more difficult than Leila's and mine. This book will help you get "smart" faster than I did—much faster.

I use real-life stories to illustrate this guide's themes and approaches to problem-solving. To protect the privacy of the elders and others in my stories, I use pseudonyms and sometimes change locations or facts that do not affect the point of the story (such as changing "son" to "daughter.")

Leila gave me permission long before she passed away to use her name and tell her story whenever it might help other families "*. . .as long as you don't tell people the secrets only my hairdresser knows.*" When I mention some of her siblings (she had 10), I also use their real names.

This book is not about "how to do it my way." Its message is not that you and your parent should live together or that you should be involved with your parent to the extent I was. It will help you regardless of where your parents live, what the situation is, and what kind of relationship you have.

Keep in mind that I do not have medical training. I am not an attorney, social worker or financial advisor. This is a guide to making informed decisions written by someone who has been where you are.

◧ *"Will our parents be able to afford staying at home?" Although this guide is not about managing finances, applying what you learn here can help your parents remain at home and protect their savings.*

Making the Most of This Guide

This book contains a wealth of information but navigating it successfully is not complicated. If you are open to new ways of thinking about problems and to taking advantage of opportunities you haven't seen before, this guide will work well for you. Always ask yourself: *"How might I apply this story or this information to my own situation?"*

The four chapters that comprise "Determining and Safeguarding 'What's Best'" are the foundation for using this book effectively and creatively. After reading them, you can pick and choose where you go next. For instance, "Helping Your Parents Long Distance" may be all you need for now.

However, reading the entire book will be helpful to you even if you and your parents are not in a difficult situation and it might prevent unforeseen nightmares. If you are already overwhelmed, finding time to read this guide from cover to cover may seem impossible. But it will be worth it. Some vital information is repeated, such as how to prevent injuries from falls.

You will learn what is "out there" to give you additional assistance with the issues that concern you and will be guided to valuable Internet sites that should be around for a long time. The book provides excellent information sources on topics not discussed at length, such as long-term care insurance. All information sources are listed in the Resource Appendix. Most are also included in the text.

Key Resources

Some organizations and government agencies are such invaluable information sources they merit listing here. They can guide you to national, state and local assistance on most topics discussed in this book. Their staff often have extensive knowledge of the communities they serve. To use these Key Resources effectively, when you are referred by one of them to another information source ask "Who would be the best person to speak to about this?"

This book refers you back to these Key Resources frequently, but do not limit your contact with them to those instances.

▶ *Area Agencies on Aging (AAAs)*
AAAs are designated by states to plan and coordinate services for older people within a specific geographic area (cities, counties, or multi-county districts). They can connect you to agencies responsible for managing local aging services, and to every resource listed below.

To find the AAA office that serves your parents' area go to the web site of the National Association of Area Agencies on Aging: www.n4a.org. Click on *Links*.

You will also find these agencies, along with other kinds of assistance, on the Eldercare Locator web site: www.eldercare.gov. You can call the Eldercare Locator at 1-800-677-1116.

▶ *Tribal aging offices*
Aging services for Native Americans are coordinated through these offices. AAAs can provide the contact information.

▶ *Independent Living Centers (ILC)*
ILCs also serve specific areas within each state and promote full participation in community life for people with disabilities. Their independent living staff members are experts on innovative ways to maintain elders' self-reliance, and are familiar with many government and local services. Staff of our local ILC were among our best sources of assistance.

The most efficient way to locate an ILC: Do an Internet search for *"Independent Living Centers"* + *name of state* (using Google, for instance).

▶ *Aging and Disability Resource Centers*
You will find ADRCs in most states. They provide "one-stop-shopping" for community services. To find a local ADRC, call your Area Agency on Aging.

▶ *Senior Centers*
  These typically are neighborhood or community centers that offer activities and services for older adults. Look in the Yellow Pages or contact an ADRC or AAA.

▶ *2-1-1 services*
  Many communities are establishing information-and- referral services that are contacted by dialing 211. Go to: www.211.org.

You will find help with searching the Internet at your public library and also in many consumer-health libraries. To find the nearest consumer-health library, use the remarkable web site of the National Institutes of Health: www.medlineplus.gov. Click on *Other Resources*, then *Libraries*.

Determining and Safeguarding "What's Best"

Chapter 1

What Is It All About?

Derailed

ᚳᚷᛤᚹ

"It's not as bad as it looks, Terry!" I was home from Washington for Thanksgiving 1983 and Leila greeted me at the door with those reassuring words. Not as bad as it looks? It looked pretty bad to me. Leila had two black eyes and a painful back injury. Her glasses were taped together. She had fainted the evening before.

Over dinner, Leila confessed that she had been fainting occasionally for more than a year. Once, her neighbors had pulled her out of the backyard bushes. She not only hadn't told me about these "little problems," she hadn't bothered her doctor with them, either.

Leila, 77, had struggled with health problems before, but this was where I said, "Life is now officially out of control." I had to do something about it before it got worse—for Leila and for me.

ᚳᚷᛤᚹ

I did "do something about it," for the next 12 years. For much of the time, especially at first, I battled for Leila's survival and my peace of mind. Her health problems were a nightmarish mix of

- ▶ fainting spells, the side effects of medications.

- ▶ permanent memory loss and confusion, not caused by Alzheimer's disease, but probably by small strokes.

- ▶ congestive heart failure (Leila's heart was not pumping efficiently).

- ▶ high blood pressure.

- ▶ a devastating bone disease, osteoporosis, that caused Leila to suffer multiple fractures. Brittle bones and fainting spells form a terrifying partnership. The worst injuries were painful "compression fractures" up and down her spine.

These health problems generated many crises. Outside forces were in charge of our lives. I worried about Leila. I worried about myself. I wondered if I would ever calm down and get a good night's sleep. I wondered when I would start living my own life again.

Back on the Tracks

Gradually, surprisingly, life got better for both of us. Life improved because Leila remained motivated to "keep on going" and I learned how to take better care of her, and myself. However, we would have remained derailed had we not learned a vital lesson: We needed help. That help came from many sources, but none more important than the kind of assistance many elders will not accept: caregivers in their homes.

Leila and I learned that "eldercare" is about much more than "being taken care of." We learned that it can be a powerful force that transforms, and often saves, the lives of frail older people. It can preserve the mental and physical health of their family members, as it did for me.

Ultimately, with lots of assistance, I was able to help Leila enjoy a fulfilling life in our home despite her physical disabilities and the memory disorder that stole her ability to manage everyday decisions. My life became simpler, less chaotic and often enjoyable. We regained control over our lives and with that control came peace of mind.

If I knew at the start what I have included in this guide we would have been back in charge of our lives sooner, more of my mother's last years would have been good ones, and I would have enjoyed much more sleep.

Keep the Flame Burning

The brighter the flame of motivation burns, the greater the power to make it through tough times.

At first, I thought that once things go wrong as you age they inevitably stay that way. I didn't realize Leila's life could get better again. To prepare for the dismal future I learned about medical services, in-home care, Meals on Wheels, wheelchairs and safety bars for bathrooms. It was useful to learn about them, but our situation didn't turn around until I understood that the key to staying in control of our lives as we age rests within ourselves. That key is motivation. If you can keep your parent's spirit alive, you can accomplish remarkable things.

I also learned how important it is to work at keeping your own flame burning. If you don't, you will lose control over your life, harming other relationships and your job performance. If you burn out, your parents are in trouble.

Remember: This is a *guide* to helping you do what is possible in your situation. It is not meant to make life more stressful if you can't go to the lengths that I did.

Try to Rekindle a Dimming Flame

Leila's love of life was the force I could call on when things were bad. Not everyone is as fortunate. I hope this guide will help you revitalize the lives of parents whose motivational flame is burning low.

Preserve the Quality of Each of Your Lives

To see what is "best," look for what it will take to keep life as good as it can be.

Assisting your parents to retain quality and dignity in their lives is the key to maintaining the flame. It keeps hope alive. With hope comes strength and remarkable power. Remembering what life was like when it was good —and seeing what it could be again—kept my mother and me motivated in times of crisis. *"Let's get out of this hospital and have lunch on our front porch"* worked more than once to get Leila back home and on her feet.

Once Leila was home, the desire to *remain* on the front porch kept her motivated to stay as strong and healthy as possible.

I made sure our lives were as normal and enjoyable as they could be. We had small dinner parties, went out to eat and took short trips. I had some social life, went on brief vacations and did other things to keep my spirits up. To preserve the quality of my life, I could not simply set it aside and live for my mother.

Being old does not mean you lose the right to decide what makes life worth living or the right to keep on living. Be cautious about deciding for an older person what "acceptable quality of life" means. You may decrease the quality of that life and put out the flame of motivation.

Even in the Darkest Times, Stay Focused on Quality of Life

Leila found that having me and other friends with her in the hospital made even the worst moments more tolerable. Life occasionally even seemed normal because we were with her. Some of you may be facing hopeless situations. Your parent may have advanced Alzheimer's disease or be in the late stage of some other terminal illness. The support and love you provide your parent in those circumstances will mean more than you can know.

Try to take pressure off yourself in heartbreaking situations. Sometimes improving quality means reducing stress and anxiety. This guide will help with this difficult task.

Many times throughout the "Leila-and-Terry Years," I was unable to follow my own advice. I would confide in close friends that I didn't see how I could keep going much longer. Usually, with their encouragement and after a good night's sleep, life looked better. The good times and the bad times taught me what I have included about coping with stress and anxiety in "Getting Strong Enough to Handle It," page 51.

I have never regretted those years. I still think of them with a sense of fulfillment. I hope this guide will help you find this sense of fulfillment as well.

Chapter 2

Preventing Problems and Overcoming Those You Can't Prevent: Eight Rules

Over the years I learned Eight Rules to follow as you help your parents keep life as good as it can be. The power of these rules has been reaffirmed many times through my experiences with other families.

Rule #1—"Old" Is Never an Acceptable Explanation

ভর্তৈ

Rob was repairing the roof of my home. When he learned about my work, he told me about his grandmother. Several years before, she had injured her hip so severely she could not walk safely even after therapy. The family and her doctor didn't want to put her through surgery because she was 82. She moved to a nursing home and used a wheelchair to get around. His grandmother lost interest in life. Her appetite diminished. Everyone was worried about her.

A new doctor took her case. He asked her why she hadn't had surgery to get back on her feet. She said she was too old. He told her she wasn't. Her heart was still strong. Rob remembered telling her, "Grandma, you could live for years.

The doctor knows what he is doing. Where do you want to spend those years?" She listened to Rob and her children and took the physician's advice. When I last saw Rob his grandmother was walking again and living in her own apartment.

ରେଛଠ

This rule applies to many situations—for instance, when we consider telling a parent "You should not do this anymore" even though she may have no significant problems with health, hearing, vision or mobility. "This" could refer to living at home, driving, taking vacation trips and other situations where safety becomes an issue. Check yourself. Why do you suggest this change? Is it strictly because of your parent's age? If so, think it over again.

Where there are legitimate safety issues, there may be less drastic ways to reduce the risk in your parents' lives. Steps to safeguard your parents' self-reliance are described throughout this book.

Rule #2—Prevention and "Old Age" Do Belong in the Same Sentence

ରେଛଠ

Leila and Virginia, one of our terrific homecare aides, were having coffee on our front porch. I asked whether they had gone on their regular morning walk, which involved getting off the porch and walking partway down the block. Leila laughed and said to Virginia, "He expects me to live forever."

ରେଛଠ

Don't ignore the obvious

As the media reminds us constantly, exercise and a healthful lifestyle can prevent many crises that hit us in old age, including strokes and heart attacks. Leila's aides and I helped her walk as much as possible to keep her strong enough to avoid more injuries from falls. She ate healthful meals. Now and then we talked her into doing safe "weightlifting" exercises approved by her physician. (See Chapter 19, "Creating a Safer Home".)

Leila's experience demonstrated what research has been telling us for some time: Even frail elders with chronic illnesses and mobility problems can benefit from carefully supervised exercise. For information on exercise appropriate for people over 50, see the Senior Health web page of the National Institutes for Health: www.nihseniorhealth.gov. Click on *Exercise for Older Adults*.

You and your parents should review the "Safety First" guidelines before they begin a new exercise routine. You will find information on healthful diets for elders at www.medlineplus.gov. Search for *Nutrition for Seniors*.

Many simple prevention steps can help your parents maintain quality of life. These two could have helped Leila remain self-reliant longer than she did.

Watch the medications

If Leila had known that fainting spells might be a side effect of her blood pressure medication, some of her worst injuries and longest hospital stays could have been avoided. Medication side effects or harmful interactions often underlie life-wrecking events.

Some health problems are caused by medications that have been prescribed inappropriately. Many older people have prescriptions from more than one doctor. This can lead to harmful treatment decisions by a physician who is unaware of this situation. Remind your parent to take all her medications with her on visits to physicians she is seeing for the first time. If she will take them with her every time she sees a doctor, new or not, even better.

Adverse reactions to prescription drugs such as dizziness, dehydration, and loss of appetite can lead to devastating consequences, including falls, depression, confusion, hallucinations and malnutrition. ("The State of

Aging and Health in America 2004," a report by the Merck Institute of Aging and Health, the Centers for Disease Control and Prevention, and the Gerontological Society of America.)

A pharmacist reminded me that over-the-counter medications, herbs and dietary supplements also can have harmful side effects and interactions. Emphasize to your parent that he should tell his physician about *everything* he is taking. Ask your pharmacist about potential problems.

For detailed information on herbs and dietary supplements, see the web site for the National Center for Complementary and Alternative Medicine: www.nccam.nih.gov. See the Resource Appendix, page 260, for more information on managing medications.

Prevent injuries from falls

Helping Leila avoid falling accidents was one of my most anxiety-producing concerns. Falls are the leading cause of accidental death among Americans age 65 and older. Fifteen to twenty-five percent of all older people who suffer hip fractures will still be in long-term care facilities a year after their accidents. ("Preventing Falls and Related Fractures," National Institute of Arthritis and Musculoskeletal and Skin Diseases. Revised August 2005.)

Many of these devastating falls occur at home. Relatively simple modifications can reduce the risk of these accidents. They include improving lighting, removing scatter rugs, and making sure your parents' floors are not slippery. For Leila's protection, we carpeted every surface in our home, including the kitchen. (Not shag.) We even put outdoor carpeting on our front porch.

▣ *There is specialized physical therapy for people with balance problems.*

Difficulty with keeping one's balance should be approached as a medical problem, not as a normal part of aging. *Always* see a physician when these problems occur. *Always* be suspicious of medications' side effects or harmful interactions. See the web site of the National Safety Council for essential information on falls prevention in and out of the home: www.nsc.org. Click on *Resources, Safety Issues*, then *Falls in the Home and Community*.

Also see the web site of the Centers for Disease Control and Prevention: www.cdc.gov. Search for *Falls Toolkit*. The Toolkit provides a checklist of steps to take and hazards to avoid.

Take advantage of the preventive services covered by Medicare

If Leila was alive today, she might be able to avoid osteoporosis, the disease that caused her bones to fracture. Now there are screening tests and treatments. Nevertheless, many older people continue to have experiences similar to Leila's. They are not aware that they have this disease until it is too late to prevent the life-changing injuries it causes.

Medicare covers only one-time preventive physical exams for new Medicare enrollees. However, in addition to osteoporosis testing it provides preventive screening for several other major diseases, including

▶ diabetes,

▶ glaucoma,

▶ heart disease, and

▶ colon, cervical, breast, vaginal and prostate cancers.

Medicare also covers vaccinations against the flu, pneumonia and hepatitis B. It does not provide a number of important preventive services, such as routine annual hearing and vision exams, nor does it cover dental services. Consequently, it is important to watch for sensory losses and to be sure your parents receive regular dental care.

More About Medicare

Your parents have a choice of two Medicare plans: Original Medicare or Medicare Advantage Plans.

Original Medicare

Original Medicare is administered by the federal government.

▸ Part A helps pay for hospital care, short-term care in nursing homes following hospitalization, some home healthcare, and hospice care. There is no premium for Part A coverage.

▸ Part B helps pay for doctors' services, diagnostic tests, medical equipment, ambulance services and other health costs. There is a monthly premium for most people.

▸ Part D covers some medication costs. (See below.)

▸ You may go to any physician who accepts Medicare payments and to any hospital.

▸ You pay a set amount each year (deductible) before Medicare payment begins. After that, Medicare pays 80 percent of your covered medical costs and you pay 20 percent (co-payment).

Physicians who do not accept the Medicare-approved payment are allowed to charge up to an additional 15 percent of the total bill. If your parent is seeking a new doctor, he might want to find out whether that physician accepts "assignment," which means she will accept what Medicare pays her. Sometimes, paying more for a particular doctor's services may be worth it.

The Medicare web site provides a list of "participating physicians" in each state. These are the doctors who accept assignment: www.medicare.gov, click on *Find a Doctor*.

▸ States have programs that pay Medicare premiums and in some cases also cover deductibles and co-insurance for people with limited assets.

▶ Medicare supplement insurance (Medigap) is private insurance that covers most Medicare co-payments and sometimes provides additional benefits. Federal and state laws set strict standards for Medigap policies to protect the consumer. Be sure your parent is not sold more than one Medigap policy. He will not need a Medigap policy if he is in the Medicaid program (page 45) or has joined a Medicare Advantage Plan.

Prescription Medication Coverage

Medicare began paying for prescription medications in January 2006 for an additional monthly premium. This prescription medication program is known as Medicare Part D or Medicare Rx. Participation in Medicare Rx is voluntary but there may be a premium penalty for delaying enrollment.

Many older adults can benefit from this program, especially those who could not otherwise afford their medications without skimping on other life necessities. People with limited income and assets are eligible for Extra Help with paying for their prescription drugs. You will find information on Extra Help on the web sites listed below.

The enrollment process can be overwhelming, primarily because the prescription drug benefit is provided through private companies that compete for the customer's business. Your parent will face what many find to be a bewildering array of prescription drug plans and may need considerable assistance. Premium costs are only one important factor to consider in choosing a plan. Other important considerations:

▶ Are all or most of your parent's medications covered by that plan?

▶ Is his pharmacy included in the plan's network?

▶ Are any of his medications covered only under special circumstances?

Be sure your parent knows that there will be a gap in coverage after his medication expenses reach a certain level. This comes as a surprise to some Medicare Rx participants.

For help with understanding Medicare Rx and choosing the best plan:

National Resources

▸ www.medicare.gov (Centers for Medicare and Medicaid Services) The Medicare helpline telephone number is 1-800-633-4227.

▸ www.aarp.org Search for *Medicare Rx*.

▸ www.ncoa.org (National Council on Aging) Search for *Medicare Rx*.

▸ www.medicareadvocacy.org (Center for Medicare Advocacy, Inc.) Click on *Medicare Part D*.

State Resources

▸ State AARP offices - www.aarp.org Click on *AARP in Your State*.

▸ Area Agencies on Aging - Staff expertise includes finding assistance for members of American Indian tribes. (See Key Resources, page 248.)

If a staff member cannot answer your questions, find out who can. Ask whether there will be Medicare Rx consumer education forums in your parents' vicinity.

Many Medicare Advantage plans (see below) also offer the prescription drug benefit but you and your parents will need to do additional homework before choosing one of these plans.

▰ *Do not wait until the last minute to help your parent find the best prescription drug plan.*

To find other prescription medication programs that help lower costs for those who meet eligibility requirements:

▸ www.benefitscheckuprx.org - National Council on Aging

▶ www.pparx.org - Partnership for Patient Assistance is an alliance of pharmaceutical companies, healthcare providers and patient advocacy organizations that assists consumers to find inexpensive medications and free healthcare clinics.

▶ www.needymeds.com - NeedyMeds is a nonprofit organization that helps people who cannot afford medicine or healthcare costs. This information includes help for some people with specific diseases and other medical conditions.

Medicare Advantage Plans

These are health plan options to Original Medicare that are approved by Medicare but are run by private companies. To participate in an Advantage Plan you must leave Original Medicare.

▶ These plans must provide all of the benefits provided under Original Medicare.

▶ Some offer more benefits and services than you will receive under Original Medicare. Service costs may be lower.

▶ Some plans restrict you to certain physicians and hospitals. Original Medicare has no such restrictions.

▶ You will continue paying the Part B premium plus the Advantage Plan's premium, should there be one.

▶ Most of these plans offer a prescription drug benefit. If you join a plan that does not offer this benefit, you may choose any of the Medicare Rx plans offered to Original Medicare participants.

▶ You must choose to receive all your Medicare benefits under an Advantage plan to get coverage under its prescription drug plan.

▶ You may not switch to another prescription drug plan while you are enrolled in an Advantage plan.

▶ If you choose an Advantage plan, you may keep your Medigap insurance but are unlikely to get any additional help from it.

You would need to continue to pay for it. You are not allowed to keep its prescription drug coverage. Before choosing Medicare Advantage, find out whether there may be obstacles to re-enrolling in your Medigap plan, if you should decide to return to Original Medicare.

Visit www.medicare.gov to learn more about Medicare Advantage plans. The Medicare helpline telephone number is 1-800-633-4227.

Before moving to a Medicare Advantage plan, no matter how attractive it may seem, it is a good idea also to call your State Health Insurance Assistance Program (SHIP). SHIP has counselors in every state and several territories that provide free one-on-one help with Medicare questions or problems.

Ask an Area Agency on Aging to help you find the state SHIP (Key Resources, page 248), or go to www.shiptalk.org.

Rule #3—Not All "Alzheimer's Disease" is Alzheimer's Disease

ᘓ৪০

Marlene attended one of my problem-solving workshops. Her mother was confused and her memory was poor. Marlene assumed it was because her mother was 80 and was in the early stages of Alzheimer's disease. She was wondering about how to choose a nursing home.

I suggested getting her mother a thorough physical examination before considering a move. She did. The doctor found that Marlene's mother had diabetes and began treatment. Within a month her mother's confusion and memory loss had disappeared and no one was talking anymore about a nursing home.

ᘔ৪০

Life-altering confusion and loss of memory are neither normal nor inevitable aspects of aging. Alzheimer's disease is not always the cause. It is one of a group of brain disorders known as "dementia." Symptoms of dementia may be caused by other, treatable, medical problems such as alcohol abuse, depression, vitamin deficiency and adverse reactions to medications.

The national Alzheimer's Association tells us all types of dementia involve mental decline that can be described in all of the following ways:

▸ Occurred from a higher level (for example, the person didn't always have a poor memory)

▸ Is severe enough to interfere with usual activities and daily life

▸ Affects more than one of the following core mental abilities:

   1. recent memory (the ability to learn and recall new information)

   2. language (the ability to write or speak, or to understand written or spoken words)

   3. visuospatial function (the ability to understand symbols, maps, etc., and the brain's ability to translate visual signals into a correct impression of where objects are in space)

   4. executive function (the ability to plan, reason, solve problems and focus on a task)

("Fact sheet: Alzheimer's disease and other dementias," Alzheimer's Association, September 15, 2006.)

▣ *Do not ignore early signs of dementia. Always obtain an informed diagnosis. Never assume that you know the causes. Stay updated on what we are learning about slowing and preventing the onset of Alzheimer's disease.*

It Wasn't "Sudden Alzheimer's"

CR80

I was on a short golf vacation in central Wisconsin, 200 miles from home. One of Leila's caregivers, Sherrie, called me: "Leila is acting very strange. She thinks she is in the hospital and keeps asking for you. We keep telling her she is home and you are golfing, but she doesn't get it. It's scary!"

Leila was taking an antibiotic for a bladder infection. I recognized the symptoms: her infection was worsening. I told Sherrie to call the emergency squad and get Leila to the hospital. I rushed home.

Several days of intravenous treatment with an antibiotic knocked out the infection and cleared Leila's mind.

CR80

I had learned from our home-health nurse that a sudden change in Leila's mental state should not be confused with dementia. This kind of problem almost always signaled another problem, such as an imbalance in her blood chemistry or the onset of an illness. There are many terms for this kind of sudden disorientation, including "delirium" and "sudden confusion."

Sudden confusion is a common and dangerous problem for hospitalized elders and also for elders in nursing homes. Sudden confusion should be treated as a medical emergency.

Check www.alz.org (national Alzheimer's Association) for information on diagnosing and treating Alzheimer's disease and other causes of dementia. You can locate your nearest Alzheimer's Association office on its web site. Staff in this office can help you find local programs and services.

The Alzheimer's Association helpline is available 24 hours a day, including weekends. Click on *Services*, then *Contact Center*. The toll-free telephone number 1-800-272-3900.

Rule #4—Loss of Interest in Life Is Not Normal at Any Age

"I have fallen and can't get up"

⋘⋙

In a class for caregivers, a man asked me: "What do you do if your father acts like he is saying, 'I have fallen and can't get up'?" I asked if he meant that his father was no longer interested in life and he said that was it.

The most telling sign was his father's loss of enthusiasm for playing cards and bowling with his pals. "He just sits there every day. That is not him." I discussed strategies for overcoming this problem, such as having his dad's friends scheme to get him back on the bowling alleys. I also suggested that his father might be in the clutches of a health crisis as devastating as many of the physical crises related to aging: depression. I wondered if he might need medical care.

The man thought that asking his dad's friends to work on getting him back to their poker games was a good starting place. He might talk to his father about seeing a physician if that strategy didn't work.

⋘⋙

Depression is an illness that sometimes accompanies the losses in old age, for instance the death of family and friends and decline of physical abilities. It is often associated with other illnesses such as Parkinson's disease and cancer. Depression frequently is misunderstood. For instance, someone who has had a "negative personality" throughout life may have been suffering from depression all along.

Depression is not a normal aspect of aging. It is not a sign of "weakness." Depression often can be treated successfully. Understanding this disease and recognizing its symptoms can literally save an elder's life. The suicide rate for Americans over 65 is disturbingly high.

For more on the causes, symptoms and treatment of depression and other mental illnesses visit the web site of the National Institute of Mental Health: www.nimh.nih.gov.

"She always gives me a boost"

⟨ßð⟩

Diane, one of Leila's personal care aides, had spent several hours with her in our home while I attended a meeting. When I returned, Diane told me, "Anyone who thinks your mom is not smart just because she can't remember things doesn't know what they are talking about." Diane had been having arguments with her mother about a family matter. Leila had helped her see her mother's point of view.

Later, when Leila and I discussed the day, she told me how much she liked Diane. "She always gives me a boost."

⟨Rßð⟩

Leila was fortunate. She never experienced depression. Her disabilities and physical discomfort, however, brought her occasional "down days" that could have multiplied in less supportive circumstances. Her mental health depended on more than "taking good care of her." The conversation with Diane had reassured Leila of her purpose in life and of her value to others.

Leila's spirits were lifted frequently by these kinds of experiences. While her caregivers were helping her bathe, fixing her lunch, or simply sharing a cup of coffee with her they would talk with Leila about their boyfriends, their families, their everyday lives. They told me how wise she was and how her insight helped them manage life's problems. The best part: they also told Leila.

Encourage your parents to remain involved in activities that add meaning to their days. Leila had been an excellent cook. Just talking with her about her famous meatloaf recipe and having her mix the ingredients helped her "still feel useful."

"What will you do after I'm gone?"

CR80

One evening Leila asked me matter-of-factly, "What will you do after I'm gone?" I was startled, but, fortunately, did not respond as I was inclined to: "Oh, Mom, I really don't want to think about it."

Instead, I told Leila I would have a very hard time for a while. I would always miss her. But I would do what she would want me to do: keep on living a full and active life. She responded, "Will you stay here? I am worried about you being alone." I told her I didn't know what I would do but that I had good friends to help me figure it out. She smiled and said I should remind her about that now and then.

Then I asked Leila a question I had not asked before: "Mom, are you afraid of dying?" Leila didn't hesitate: "I believe there is a plan for all of us. I was OK before I got here and I will be OK after I go. I will hate to leave you but I am not afraid of what comes next." Then she said, "But we can worry about that later. How about going out to dinner?" Leila and I went out to dinner for several more years and now and then reassured each other we would both be OK after she was gone.

CR80

This conversation enriched my understanding of what an adult child can do to help a parent remain engaged in life in old age. Leila had been unusually quiet for a couple of days before this discussion. Her mood was lighter afterward. It was therapeutic for her to discuss a topic I thought she would have preferred to avoid. What might have been upsetting to Leila a few years before comforted her at 85.

Her aides and I recognized that Leila benefited not only from talking about the realities of the future but also from telling us about the past. She had happy memories and it made her happy to share them. Her mother and one of her brothers had "died before their time." She needed to tell us about these painful experiences as well. Look for cues indicating that your parent wishes to talk about something you assumed she would rather avoid.

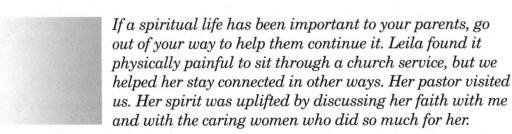

If a spiritual life has been important to your parents, go out of your way to help them continue it. Leila found it physically painful to sit through a church service, but we helped her stay connected in other ways. Her pastor visited us. Her spirit was uplifted by discussing her faith with me and with the caring women who did so much for her.

Rule #5—Rehabilitation Is Not Only for the Young

ೞഽ

Leila was hospitalized with a fractured pelvis a few months after we moved back to Wisconsin from Washington in 1985. She was 79. Because she was injured so severely, I feared that Leila's life would never be the same again. I called Dr. Swenson, an acquaintance who specialized in the medical care of older adults. I told her my fears and how helpless I felt. She told me: "I have seen badly injured and very ill older people rehabilitate quite nicely with time. Don't give up." With this hopeful advice in mind and with physical therapy at home, Leila recovered and went on with life.

ೞഽ

Don't count your parents out when they are down. They may well be capable of "rehabilitating quite nicely with time." Skilled physical therapy often works wonders even for people well past 90.

Remember, there is specialized rehabilitation therapy for people with balance problems.

Many elders with significant medical, mobility or sensory problems can remain quite self-reliant. They can stay in control of their lives, as long as they are able to use good judgment—and as long as we let them.

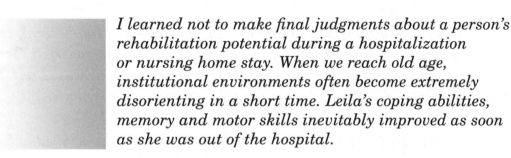

I learned not to make final judgments about a person's rehabilitation potential during a hospitalization or nursing home stay. When we reach old age, institutional environments often become extremely disorienting in a short time. Leila's coping abilities, memory and motor skills inevitably improved as soon as she was out of the hospital.

Rule # 6—Preoccupation with Safety Can Be Risky

Aunt Alvira's graduate course on living with acceptable risk

ೞ

My Aunt Alvira was unconscious for days, first in a hospital, then a nursing home. The doctors and staff thought she had suffered a stroke. Then "Alvira's miracle" occurred. She woke up. Because she was tough and stubborn, Aunt Alvira returned home, over the protests of family members, including me. (I protested from long distance since I was still living in Washington.)

A nursing home social worker helped Aunt Alvira find what she needed to remain relatively self-reliant. She paid a neighbor to assist her with bathing, shopping and laundry. A nurse checked on her weekly. Aunt Alvira continued physical therapy. She told me how impressed the therapist was with how quickly she improved.

I visited her a few weeks after she got home. "She has improved?" I remarked to myself. "What was she like three weeks ago?" Aunt Alvira moved around by staggering from doorjamb to doorjamb, stopping to lean on whatever piece of furniture she found in her path. I covered my eyes when she went upstairs to bed. She would cling to the railing and haul herself to the top, stair by agonizing stair.

I tried to talk Aunt Alvira into sleeping downstairs. "Aunt Alvira, why do you insist on going up those stairs every night?" She replied: "Well, Terry Boy, because that's where my bedroom is. If I get tired on the way up, I rest. It's the only exercise I get. Please don't try to take my stairs away from me."

I surrendered and stopped bugging Aunt Alvira. She continued to haul herself up those stairs and to stagger around her home. Now and then she fell but was never seriously injured. We questioned her judgment once more: "Now isn't it time to move to someplace safer?" Aunt Alvira thought otherwise. She told me she chose to live as the lyrics from an old song suggested, "I pick myself up, dust myself off, and start all over again."

Some of her former piano students visited Aunt Alvira regularly. Sometimes they brought their children. They always brought her pleasure. Aunt Alvira spent many hours in her living room easy chair, "watching the world go by." She dined on ham slices, fruit, and TV dinners. She lived like this, stubbornly and contentedly, until she left us one day as she sat in her easy chair watching children play in the schoolyard across the street. Aunt Alvira was 94. It had been six years since she left the nursing home.

CRYED

At first, I thought that what I was learning from Aunt Alvira was specific only to her. No one was going to tell her how to live her life, so we might as well let her live it. I finally realized she was teaching me much more than that. She was giving me a graduate course on the dignity and power of being "allowed" to live with life-saving risk.

Aunt Alvira's choice would not be the right one for everyone, especially older people who are more fragile and less determined than she was. But it was undoubtedly the best choice for Aunt Alvira. She would have been miserable anywhere else. Her home kept her alive.

Safer sometimes isn't

જી&

David called to tell me, "I think I just made a mistake you would have talked me out of." His father was experiencing difficult medical problems. David had him move to a nursing home near him. "I thought he would be better off there but he has already fallen and broken a rib. So now they don't have him walk to the dining room. They take him in a wheelchair. He has lost a lot of strength he could not afford to lose. I am working harder now (on his dad's situation) than before he went into the home."

I suggested helping his dad return to the apartment where he had been living and providing him with more help. However, David was in over his head. He could not think about helping his father move again. He asked if I could help him improve his father's situation in the nursing home. I honored his request, while each of us continued to wish he had called me sooner.

જી&

Living with some risk can be the least risky option. As David discovered, persuading a parent to move to a nursing home for safety reasons can boomerang. Nursing home staff help many residents a day. They cannot continually watch over individuals. It is often difficult for them to find time for assisting residents to walk or exercise.

The resulting loss of residents' physical strength and balance can lead quickly to injuries and increased disability. Instant depression is not uncommon, either. Family members can help reduce these kinds of problems with frequent visits but David did not wish to be involved in his father's life to that extent.

Your crystal ball may be flawed

Pressuring a parent to move to head off something that may or may not lie ahead can snuff out the motivation flame overnight. Would moving decrease your parent's control over her life? If so, it needs to be weighed carefully against the benefits. Preoccupation with safety not only can reduce your parents' enjoyment of life, it can drain unnecessarily their savings—or yours. Sometimes a move is the best idea. Sometimes it isn't.

Ultimately, no one can tell you what to do in tricky situations

. . . and it is not my intent to do it here. I hope this guide will help you and your parents weigh all your options before you make decisions about issues of safety.

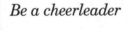

Be a cheerleader

Knowing you are with them all the way can be a powerful energizer for frail elders who can continue living on their own with some assistance. A few months after Aunt Alvira "converted" me she told me, "Thank you for being in my corner. We need cheerleaders."

Rule # 7—Your Parents and You Are the Experts

"Just get me home"

ᑓᔑᐤ

Throughout the hospital stay that I described in Rule #5, Leila was unable to stand without two people assisting her. While I agonized over what to do after she was discharged (Rehabilitation hospital? Nursing home?) she would tell me "Just get me home. I will be OK." Up to the time Dr. Swenson assured me that Leila might well rehabilitate successfully, I was certain I would not be able to take Leila home until and unless she was back on her feet.

After my talk with the doctor, Leila and I decided to go home and see what would happen. I scheduled 24-hour care, took her home and left on a short business trip. I checked in periodically. Leila was making some progress but still required two people to help her stand. When I returned, there was Leila, walking to the living room, one person at her side. "Mom, you're walking!" She looked at me with a quizzical mile. "How else can I get to my armchair?" I did not question her logic.

I marveled that Leila knew the solution to this problem from the first day she entered the hospital. "I will be OK once I get back home." This experience changed our lives and was the foundation of my approach to the crises that followed. Whenever Leila was hospitalized, I would focus both of us on getting back to our living room and our beloved front porch. It worked for nine more years, until the last few months of Leila's life.

ᑓᔑᐤ

If you make decisions without considering what keeps your parents engaged in life, the results usually will be unfortunate—for your parent and for you.

Age, frailty and illness do not add up necessarily to "unable to decide what is best." Once their family members listened to Leila and my Aunt Alvira, things went well. Sometimes, as in Rob's story about his grandmother, we have to assist our aging loved ones to see what is best by helping them see what is possible.

Don't expect professionals such as physicians or staff of residential facilities to decide how and where your parents should live. They are often valuable allies but their job is to provide services and discuss options, not tell you what to do. No responsible physician or other professional would suggest otherwise.

There are many situations in which children must become the "experts" on what a parent should not do. For instance, had I been unable to ensure Leila's safety at home, I would have had to try to steer her toward other kinds of living arrangements.

What if a parent will not listen? Try to apply the strategies I suggest in Chapter 3: "How Do I Help My Parents If I Can't Get Through to Them?" and in Chapter 7 on assisting parents from a distance. Sometimes you may have to accept a parent's unwise decision with potentially nightmarish consequences and hope for the best. Old age, alone, is not reason enough to strip him of the right to make a poor choice. However, if a parent is no longer capable of understanding the implications of his decisions you might have to resort to a guardianship proceeding to protect him from harm. (See page 43.)

Rule # 8—*The Labels Must Go*

Leila and I learned that age discrimination is not limited to employment. Labels such as "aging woman with dementia" often blurred the fact that my mother was Leila Lynch—a person with feelings and rights. These kinds of labels made life more difficult for both of us. Sometimes they made life hazardous for Leila. I don't mean to imply that anyone labeled her purposely. It's just how it was. I know. I was one of "them" at first. It took a caring doctor who saw past Leila's labels to set me straight.

"Leila told me she hurt"

ᎴᏇᏇᏇ

A few months after our return to Wisconsin, Leila was injured while I was traveling. Soon after entering the hospital, she began physical therapy. She told me over the telephone how painful it was to walk. I thought she wasn't able to understand that the therapist knew what was best for her. The labels "old" and "confused" controlled how I saw this situation. I told Leila to stay tough and not "baby" herself. However, when I returned I saw how agonizing it was for Leila to walk. I stopped her "therapy" session and went looking for answers.

Before I could request more tests, her physician, Dr. Johnson, who had been out of town, stormed down the hospital corridor. He was furious. "I ordered additional X-rays. They have been walking your mother on a fractured pelvis!" He apologized profusely. I asked him why he ordered the X-rays. He looked at me as though he could not understand my question and replied, "Leila told me she hurt."

ᏇᏇᏇ

If others are to do well by our parents, we must make sure our parents' best interest is never blurred by harmful labels.

Chapter 3

How Can I Help My Parents If I Can't Get Through to Them?

ထာ

A physician told me of a presentation she had given to a women's group. Most of its members were over 70. Her topic was preventing injuries from falls. She asked how many in her audience had fallen within the past year. No one raised her hand. Then she asked how many really had fallen but didn't want to admit it, especially to their children, for fear of going to a nursing home. Half the room raised their hands.

ထာ

The Thanksgiving trip to Wisconsin that awakened me to the severity of Leila's health problems also opened my eyes to why she hadn't told me what was going on. When I learned she had been fainting, I got angry with her for not telling her physician, and her son. Then Leila got angry. "If you don't want to help me, then don't! I am not asking you to do anything about it am I?"

I told her I was upset that she wasn't taking care of herself. It wasn't because I didn't want to help her. I asked Leila to return to Washington with me to find the answers to her medical problems. The next day, after cooling off, she said she would.

The miles between us were not the only reason I hadn't known the extent of Leila's health problems. Her anxiety about the consequences of telling me, or anyone else, was an even bigger communication barrier. Leila thought she was on an unavoidable slide. She chose to ignore problems that were medically treatable partly because she feared they weren't and did not want to learn the frightful truth.

Leila also was worried that I would want her in a "safer" place—a nursing home. She told me later there was yet another reason for not asking me for help: "I didn't want to be a burden."

Some suggestions for getting past these kinds of common communication barriers:

Stay Strategic: Fit Your Actions to Your Goal

Your goal should be to convince your parents to involve you (within reason) in helping them maintain quality of life. It should never be to prove to them you are right and they are wrong for the sake of being "right."

Assure Your Parents You Are with Them All the Way
(The strategic step that paves the way for the others)

Before the Thanksgiving visit I had been going blithely along, seldom discussing the future with Leila. When we did talk about it, our conversations were about finances, not health. I hesitated to discuss what might happen should she become disabled or ill. I didn't want to upset her. Because we didn't talk about these things, Leila didn't know I was committed to helping her in any circumstance. Consequently, she avoided telling me about problems she otherwise might have brought up.

Telling parents you want to assist them to preserve their well-being can determine how they view and respond to problems that may come along. If they know your solutions to these problems do not automatically include a move to a nursing home, they may be more likely to confide in you.

If your parents resist sharing their concerns about the future, do not force this discussion. If one parent seems more open to a conversation than the other, try a private chat with that parent. If another family member might get through to your parents more effectively, try that approach.

Share with Your Parents This Guide's Hopeful Message

Even a brief discussion of the uplifting messages in Chapter Two's "Eight Rules" can put them at ease.

Make a Full Disclosure Agreement

Once your parents understand they do not face an inevitably bleak future, they should be more likely to communicate their problems and concerns. Ask them to keep you informed on events that might affect their self-reliance, for instance beginning new medications.

Don't Try to Take Over

Avoid treating your parents like children

Nothing will alienate them more quickly. Help them through problems with their dignity intact.

Be careful not to cause your parents more anxiety

They may be paralyzed by fear of the future. Loss of physical and perhaps mental capabilities may be affecting them. Dear friends may have died. Make clear you are not trying to take something else away from them. You are committed to helping them retain as much of their world as possible.

Don't bombard your parents with all the problems you think should be fixed

It is likely to overwhelm them. Be selective and strategic.

Try not to let your emotions interfere with your goals

If your parents frustrate you, don't blow up. It will push them farther away.

Be aware of your motives

Are you using a particular situation to carry out another "agenda," such as making your life easier or getting back at your dad for something that happened when you were a kid?

Remember that stubborn is not helpful

Are there ways your parents think or behave that you will not change through direct confrontation? Stop confronting them. For instance, if your dad will never take advice from anyone, don't try to force it on him.

Be Creative

അ

Ellen was frustrated. Her father had died recently. She was trying to help her mother get her life organized. Her mother declined Ellen's help. But she accepted her granddaughter's ideas and assistance. Ellen decided to just enjoy being with her mother.

അ

CROKO

Pete was recovering from surgery. He loved to walk, but his wife was not able to help him. He said he would never accept assistance from an outsider. I visited him with Cathy, a friend of mine who also happened to do caregiving work. Pete enjoyed his time with her. I called him later to ask if he would like to have Cathy help him once in a while. She started the next day.

CROKO

Don't Give In to Family Decision-Making Paralysis

CROKO

Although Doris was 85, she remained fit and active. Consequently, after she underwent surgery for breast cancer, the doctors recommended the same chemotherapy treatment they gave to younger patients. Unfortunately, long after her treatment ended she remained weak and confused. Her doctors could not explain what had happened. Her sister, Carmen, had Doris move in with her temporarily.

I asked Carmen to consider taking her sister to an excellent medical clinic in Chicago, 20 miles from their suburban home. Carmen was overwhelmed and incapable of acting on my suggestions. Her two sons agreed that the clinic was a good idea, but "Aunt Doris will resist this." I pointed out the likely consequences of not figuring out what was going on with their aunt and told them I would help them.

Unfortunately, this family never got past the barriers to seeking an accurate diagnosis. Within a few months, Doris was no longer walking. She slumped further into confusion and spent her last year in a nursing home.

CROKO

People in dire circumstances, who may have a way out, sometimes don't do anything. There are many explanations, such as not wanting to hurt a doctor's feelings or believing that there is no hope. Giving in to reactions such as these can destroy years of a person's life or end it prematurely.

Chapter 4

Advance Planning: A *Very* Good Idea

Legal and financial planning arrangements can help preserve the quality of your parents' lives in difficult circumstances. Some require your parents to authorize others to make certain decisions on their behalf. I will summarize the arrangements Leila and I used, and describe some others. Most states have their own laws governing delegations of authority.

▣ *Decision-making power should never be delegated to anyone who is not reliable and ethical beyond question.*

Financial and Property Management Authorizations

Leila's memory disorder did not take away her right, or her capacity, to decide what was best for her. However, she had difficulty managing her checkbook and making financial decisions. We used a general power of attorney (POA) arrangement to overcome these problems.

General POA is a written authorization in which a person (the "grantor" or the "principal") designates another (the "agent") to act on his or her behalf. The principal can delegate limited authority or grant broad powers to the agent.

Examples:

▸ You grant a friend the authority to sell your car for you. (Limited power)

▸ You authorize your agent to manage your financial affairs. (Broad power)

Setting up a POA does not limit the grantor's power to make his own decisions on the matters delegated to the agent. The agent is not entitled to override the grantor's wishes.

Durable Power of Attorney (DPOA or DPA)

General power of attorney was too limited for Leila and me. It ends when the person who authorizes it is no longer competent to make decisions on her own behalf. A DPOA arrangement gave me broad powers to manage Leila's finances and extended my authority to those times when she was incapable of thinking clearly. Another option for Leila would have been to grant me DPOA for *only* those times.

An attorney or bank officer can tell you how DPOA arrangements are created and terminated where your parents live. Their bank may require its customers to use its own DPOA form. Consider involving a lawyer in establishing your DPOA, as we did. Our attorney tailored the DPOA document to fit our situation and made certain that Leila understood the extent of the authority she was granting me.

Arrangements that delegate limited power

▸ *Joint tenancy and dual signature bank accounts*
In most cases these accounts must be established before the onset of incapacity. In joint tenancy arrangements, either individual on the account may write checks or withdraw money. Dual bank accounts

require the signatures of both account holders. One drawback: A dual account is frozen when one of the account holders dies.

▶ *Representative payee for government benefits*
This arrangement authorizes a relative, friend, or other trusted person to receive Social Security payments on behalf of a beneficiary who is unable to manage his finances. The representative must use these funds for the personal care and well-being of the beneficiary. The federal Social Security Administration requires periodic reports on how these funds are managed. Call your local SSA office for information on this arrangement.

▶ *Bill-Paying Services*
Private bill-paying services can eliminate many life-disrupting "I'm certain I took care of that" incidents. Some communities have money-management programs that offer this service. Many utility companies have arrangements to assist elders to pay their bills. Check with Area Agencies on Aging and family services and aging services agencies.

There are many other ways to assist your parents to protect and manage their financial assets. Some are discussed later in this chapter.

Advance Directives for Healthcare

When Leila was ill or in pain due to an injury, she was usually too confused to guide decisions regarding her healthcare. We set up an arrangement that enabled me to make decisions for her in those circumstances.

Healthcare Power of Attorney (or Medical POA)

Wisconsin law allows individuals to grant healthcare POA without an attorney's involvement. Friends witnessed our agreement. Leila's POA described specifically how she wished to be cared for in a variety of health crises. For instance, she did not want her life prolonged by emergency care or artificial life supports if she was terminally ill or in a "persistent vegetative state." Leila specified her wishes in a conversation with me guided by a discussion booklet I obtained at a local hospital.

This advance directive also empowered me to make treatment decisions in any situation for which Leila had not provided clear directions. She trusted that I would always ask myself: "What would Leila do if she was capable of making these decisions?" regardless of how difficult emotionally it might be for me to follow her wishes. Chapter 10, starting at page 105, provides illustrations related to acting in a parent's best interest in difficult circumstances.

A medical POA takes effect *only* when the patient is incapable of making informed decisions in his best interest. The laws of each state govern how incapacity shall be determined. In Wisconsin, two physicians or a physician and a psychologist must agree in writing that the patient cannot direct his own care.

If possible, your parents should designate more than one healthcare agent. They should also make clear which agent has final authority in case of disagreement. If your parents do not wish to delegate this power, their best choice might be a living will.

Leila's healthcare power of attorney enabled me to preserve the quality of her life for as long as possible and to ensure that her death was dignified and comfortable.

The Living Will

Leila had the option of preparing a living will. This advance directive guides physicians' decisions about the use of life-sustaining procedures when the patient is terminally ill. A living will does not empower another to make decisions on behalf of the patient. Some states combine the living will with a medical POA. If your parent has both, be sure they do not conflict.

Anyone who provides healthcare to your parent should have a copy of his medical advance directive. Your parent may modify either directive at any time, even during a hospitalization, as long as he is competent. Attorneys and providers of healthcare will be able to advise you on whether it may be desirable for your parents to have both kinds of advance directives.

Attorneys, medical clinics, hospitals and nursing homes will have forms that comply with the laws of the state where your parents reside.

▸ *When Leila's serious health problems began, she had no advance directive. This made life more difficult than it needed to be and potentially more hazardous for Leila. For instance, today, without her direction Leila's physicians might have felt obliged to fight for her life no matter what I told them about what Leila considered her best interest.*

Guardianship

Guardianship may be a family's only option if a parent becomes permanently incapacitated and power of attorney arrangements have not been established. A guardianship is a relationship in which one person (the guardian) is appointed by a court to make decisions on behalf of another person (the ward), after the court has determined that person to be incompetent.

Establishing POA arrangements ensured that I would not have had to humiliate my mother in a court guardianship proceeding and that a court would never oversee my relationship with her.

For more on all forms of powers of attorney and on guardianships, see the web page of the American Bar Association: www.abanet.org/aging.

Authorizations for Release of Medical Information

The federal Health Insurance Portability and Accountability Act (HIPAA) has made it more difficult for family and friends to learn about the condition or treatment of a patient than it used to be. HIPAA requirements forbid providers of healthcare from disclosing any medical or health-related information to *anyone* who has not been properly authorized to receive this information. "Anyone" includes one's children, siblings or even a spouse.

A medical POA does not authorize healthcare providers to release information to you unless your parent is incapacitated. This means that you might rush to your parent's side in the hospital and be informed that physicians and nurses may not discuss your parent's situation with you, unless he is present, because he has not permitted them to do so in writing. Verbal permission would probably work in the immediate circumstance but don't expect it to solve the authorization problem permanently.

To avoid HIPAA headaches, your parent will need to complete a form authorizing the release of medical information to you and to anyone else who should have access to it. Be sure this form is in your parent's medical file and that you have a copy. Once you have this authority you will be better able to help direct your parent's care, even from long distance.

While most of us don't like to think about these kinds of advance planning issues, this is another instance in which a little prevention goes a long way toward avoiding problems later on.

"Will I Be Able to Afford Getting Old?"

A friend in my favorite coffee shop asked this question. She was wondering whether she would be able to afford long-term care, which commonly refers to the variety of services, such as homecare, that one may need for an extended period due to chronic illness or prolonged disability—the kinds of assistance and services described in this guide. Her parents' financial situation was her immediate concern.

This summarizes my reply and the following conversation:

▶ Many of us will never need long-term care, but we should plan as though we will.

▶ Neither your parents nor you can count on government long-term help with living anywhere other than nursing homes.

> ▶ Ample financial resources can make an enormous difference in quality of life in old age.

"But doesn't Medicare help?"

Medicare is a federal government health insurance program. It pays for limited assistance from nurses and home-health aides only when "skilled care" has been ordered by a physician. Skilled care refers to services such as physical therapy or intravenous medical treatment. Medicare covers short stays in nursing homes after hospitalizations, and it is only for those who need skilled care.

Medicaid helps, but not enough

Medicaid is a government program that provides medical benefits to certain groups of people with low incomes and limited assets. Each state establishes its own Medicaid program under broad federal government guidelines. Leila qualified in Wisconsin because of her financial situation, her age and her disabilities.

The good news about Medicaid is that it is there. The bad news is that, as Leila had to do, you have to spend most of your life savings in order to qualify. And, although Medicaid entitles you to nursing home care, it provides limited assistance to people who wish to remain at home.

Medicaid also is notorious for under-reimbursing nursing homes, homecare agencies, hospitals and other providers of healthcare. Consequently, it can be difficult to find a preferred nursing home placement and sometimes homecare for a person whose payment source is Medicaid. Some physicians will not accept Medicaid patients due to this low rate of reimbursement. Leila had to find another dentist once she became Medicaid-eligible.

Don't misunderstand. Medicaid can be an important piece of the long-term care puzzle for those with minimal resources. Medicaid covers most healthcare costs not paid for by Medicare. Limited help at home might be all that is needed, especially if an elder has assistance from friends or family members.

Understanding Medicaid is never easy. There are many resources to help you determine whether your parent is eligible in his state and, if not, what steps he might take to become Medicaid-eligible. I would start with your parents' Area Agency on Aging, Aging and Disability Resource Center or Independent Living Center for guidance to reliable information and assistance related to Medicaid eligibility. (Key Resources, page 248.)

Also ask these organizations for referrals to ethical attorneys well-versed in Medicaid law. I was guided to expert and reliable attorneys in Wisconsin by contacting my state Disability Rights agency. You can find your parents' state agency at the web site of the National Disability Rights Network: www.ndrn.org.

The web page of the National Institutes of Health provides consumer-friendly information on Medicaid: www.medlineplus.gov. Search for *Medicaid*.

There is additional information on the Medicaid program in Chapter 18.

▷ *If your parent has few assets, contact a Medicaid expert to learn whether she may be Medicaid-eligible. I wish I had done that for Leila. I learned, too late, that Medicaid rules would have allowed her to purchase certain items she needed to attain eligibility. Those items included a new armchair and a television set for her bedroom. She also could have paid medical bills in advance.*

▷ *Be wary about transferring your parent's assets to you or a sibling to qualify him for Medicaid. Program rules are tougher and more complex than some "asset protection" seminars lead you to believe. There are strict financial penalties for transferring assets or property simply to qualify a parent for Medicaid. And if gifting assets to adult children might put out or diminish the flame, encouraging your parents to do it anyway can be extraordinarily destructive.*

"So what do you suggest I do?"

Advance planning for finances is as essential as it is for the other topics discussed in this chapter, regardless of income or amount of savings.

If you prefer do-it-yourself:

- ▶ Try AARP's web site: www.aarp.com. Click on *Money and Work*, then *Financial Planning and Retirement*.

- ▶ See the Medicare program's information and tools for helping you and your parent plan: www.medicare.gov. Click on *Long-term care*.

Leila and I wanted planning assistance. We benefited from the services of a Certified Financial Planner (CFP). A CFP is one of a variety of professionals trained to assist you with various aspects of managing your money. Others include accountants and estate-planning attorneys.

▣ *If you want help with planning, still do your homework. Do not leave important decisions to even the most reliable and competent professionals. The people you want to work with will be those who encourage and assist you to be an informed consumer.*

Our planner, Michele, was a model for what you should look for from any financial professional.

- ▶ She had an outstanding reputation.

- ▶ She was dedicated to helping us maintain the best possible quality of life, not to "selling" us anything.

- ▶ Michele respected Leila's wishes as much as she respected mine.

- ▶ We never felt pressured by her.

- ▶ She guided us to decisions that were in our best interests.

Michele suggested that we also consult with an estate-planning attorney. He helped us set up a trust for Leila's remaining assets that enabled me to avoid some probate-related expenses after Leila passed away. The Certified Financial Planner Board of Standards, Inc. provides information about financial professionals and their areas of expertise. The Board's web page includes information on how to check on credentials and on the kinds of questions to ask of any potential adviser: www.cfp.net.

Be sure no disciplinary actions have been taken against someone you may be considering. Click on *How to Choose a Planner*, then on *How to Check on Disciplinary History*.

⊡ *Unless you are as certain as we were about the ethics and expertise of a financial professional, keep looking.*

"What do you think of Long-Term Care Insurance?"

Purchasing insurance to help you pay for the costs of long-term care can be an important part of your financial plan. Deciding whether you should is complicated. The variety of options and choices can be bewildering. You should not buy a long-term care insurance policy until you are a very well educated consumer. This decision should be made as part of an informed financial planning process. People who are in the Medicaid program will not need this insurance.

The National Association of Insurance Commissioners (NAIC) sets out these basic rules in "A Shopper's Guide to Long-term Care Insurance":

You should NOT buy long-term care insurance if

▶ You can't afford the premiums.

▶ You have limited assets.

▶ Your only source of income is a Social Security benefit or Supplemental Security Income (SSI).

▶ You often have trouble paying for utilities, food, medicine, or other important needs.

▶ You are on Medicaid.

You should CONSIDER buying long-term care insurance if

▶ You have significant assets and income.

▶ You want to protect some of your assets and income.

▶ You can pay premiums, including possible premium increases, without financial difficulty.

▶ You want to stay independent of the support of others.

▶ You want the flexibility of choosing care in the setting you prefer or in which you will be most comfortable.

An excellent financial planner reminded me that affordability is sometimes best determined in a comprehensive planning process that involves a careful look at the consumer's priorities.

Contact the office of your state insurance commissioner for a copy of the NAIC guide and for other information to help you and your parents work through this difficult decision. Each state also has a State Health Insurance Assistance Program (SHIP) that provides Medicare beneficiaries with information and counseling on insurance questions related to healthcare and long-term care.

You can find the office of your state insurance commissioner at the NAIC web site: www.naic.org. Click on *NAIC states and jurisdictions*. To find your state SHIP go to www.shiptalk.org, contact your Key Resources, page 248, or call the Medicare helpline at 1-800-633-4227.

▣ *Make certain that any policy you consider*

▶ *is offered by a reliable insurance company with substantial assets*

> ▶ supports the kinds of creative strategies you find in this book for assisting your parents to remain at home

Perhaps your home can help fund the future

Home Equity Conversion (a reverse mortgage) enables you to convert your home's value into cash without having to move or repay the loan until you sell the home, leave it, or transfer its title. To be eligible for most reverse mortgages you must own your home and be 62 or older. Your income level doesn't matter.

There are several reverse mortgage options and ways in which the cash can be paid out to you. And, of course, there are various drawbacks. The Center for Home Equity Conversion provides the details, help with comparing loans and guidance in finding one: www.reverse.org.

For information on loans available to people with low incomes and people with disabilities use the Benefits Checkup tool provided by the National Council on Aging: www.benefitscheckup.org.

Look to your community for cost-saving services that support long-term care

Help with long-term care is not inevitably expensive. See page 154, for more programs and services that can help frail elders, and their adult children, remain in control of their lives.

Getting Strong Enough to Handle It

Chapter 5

Take Advantage of Your Natural Resources

Unclutter Your Mind

You may be where I was at first: lost in a blizzard of concerns. Lesser worries seem as urgent as the most serious health problems. It is difficult to see where to start. Don't try to tackle everything at once. Once you clear your mind even a little, you will be able to proceed more efficiently.

Delegate responsibility and ask for help.

To unscramble your overloaded brain, get others to take some of your responsibilities. For instance, turn cooking duties over to your husband and children. They will survive. Ask your computer-genius daughter to help you find information about a parent's medical problems. Look for every opportunity to delegate tasks, even minor ones. Each time you do your anxiety will decrease.

Let someone help you think.

Life became less stressful, and my brain less foggy, as soon as I let a trusted friend help me with problem-solving. Don't rule out using the telephone. A friend doesn't have to be in your living room to be a good partner in clutter reduction.

Sort things out.

CRSO

Larry asked me to help him. His dad lived in Seattle, Larry in Wisconsin. These were his concerns.

▶ *His father's hearing was impaired.*

▶ *His father had been fainting occasionally.*

▶ *The home his father lived in was "full of dust balls."*

▶ *Larry said his father was "increasingly forgetful." He was afraid his dad would forget food on the stove and burn the house down. He couldn't hear timers.*

▶ *Larry was concerned about his relationship with his sister. She was upset that he didn't want to have their father move to a nursing home.*

▶ *Larry felt "a little guilty" about what he would never do: Invite his dad to live with his family. They never had a good relationship, but Larry still wanted to do as much as he could long distance.*

CRSO

This is how we figured out what to work on right away.

What could be set aside for a while?

▶ *Dust!*
I observed that "a house full of dust balls" seemed to be causing Larry as much anxiety as "Dad fainted when he stood up after

dinner." He laughed and agreed that these problems seemed to be equally stress-producing. He didn't know where to start. We began with the dust balls. His father had lived with them since Larry's mother died; he could live with them a while longer. We had to talk about this for a few minutes before Larry decided to let it go for the moment. He started to relax.

▶ *A stressful relationship*
Larry had been losing sleep over his difficulties with his sister. As he was determined to try to help his dad stay home, I wondered if he also could let this problem go for a while. It was burdening him so much he couldn't think clearly. Larry agreed that once we had a plan his sister might calm down. Her overwhelming concern was her father's safety.

What could Larry let go of altogether?

▶ *Guilt*
Guilt is one of the family member's worst enemies. It can be so consuming it is impossible to get down to business. Larry didn't need to chew on this problem now. I pointed out that he was going out of his way for his father. He was caring for him, not letting him down. Sometimes a family member needs "permission" to let go of guilt.

What should be Larry's priorities?

What Larry should work on first was now more obvious to him. He had to focus on his father's health and safety problems, and he was in better shape to do it than he had been 30 minutes earlier. The story of Larry and his dad continues in Chapter 8, "Common Sense Works."

🔁 *Do you really have to get rid of those magazines right now? Or clean your mother's kitchen? Can't you put off worrying about your father's safety at home until after you help him through hip surgery? Are you feeling guilty about something that you don't need to do or fix? These are the kinds of questions to ask of anyone finding her way through the problem-solving maze.*

Tap Into the Power of Community

Life in the Lynch household improved as Leila's medical care and my problem-solving improved. Nothing was more important to us, however, than our allies—those people with an emotional investment in what I was doing for my mother and in her battle to remain in her home. Over time, we found many friends who would go out of their way to help us.

Whether you are involved substantially in your parents' lives or are just concerned about their future, getting someone else involved can work wonders. It may not be as difficult as it seems. Your allies can help you and your parents avoid some problems and can reduce the impact of those you can't avoid.

We were lucky. Some of our neighbors were invested from the start. They brought us meals. A few helped us on short notice—for instance staying with Leila when I had to go to a spur-of-the-moment meeting.

Just say "Yes."

At first, when someone offered to do something for us, such as grocery shopping, I was reluctant to accept. "Thanks, but we are getting along fine." After I was worn down far enough, I started answering, "That would be wonderful!" Once I learned to accept help, I realized I could ask for it from my true allies. Accepting help when it was offered, and daring to ask for it (within reason) were two big steps in improving the quality of our lives. I wished I had started saying yes sooner.

One ally is a good start.

If you can't think of several potential allies, don't be discouraged. Even one person who is committed to helping you and your parent can lift your spirits. You no longer are alone.

Long distance works fine.

If you live some distance from your parents, would one of their friends, neighbors or other relatives help them and stay in touch with you? One of the most important conversations I ever had about my mother's medical care was long distance to Dr. Swenson, the physician who gave me hope at a difficult time. (See Chapter 2, page 24.)

"But what if there is no one? What do I do then?"

▶ *Try caregiver support groups sooner rather than later.*

 C3&O

I had begun a problem-solving discussion with a small group in a church meeting room. The participants had exchanged a few stories about the stress related to caregiving. A woman who was caring for her mother raised her hand. Her comment made my evening. She said, "I already feel better because now I realize I'm not alone. It is such a relief!"

C3&O

In many communities, churches and other organizations sponsor meetings for family caregivers. You are likely to find rewarding and calming relationships in these groups. Try them even if you already have allies. No one can better understand what you and your parent are experiencing. There are support groups specifically for family caregivers of people with Alzheimer's disease and other disorders that cause dementia.

Besides emotional support, group meetings provide useful information on concerns such as how to find in-home help or a good physician. If one group isn't helpful, try another. Support groups are sponsored by a variety of community organizations. Their meetings are often advertised in newspapers.

Internet caregiver support groups enable you to "talk" with other family caregivers across the United States. You can discuss your situation, vent your emotions and get ideas from others. You remain anonymous if you wish. The Internet might be worth trying even if you are not housebound. (Resource Appendix, page 266.)

▶ *Hook up with individual caregivers*

You might develop a friendship with someone in a support group. That friendship could work better for you than groups do, even if you communicate with each other mainly by telephone.

I developed mutually supportive relationships with family caregivers who were not caring for parents. For instance, I networked my way to Mike through a home-health nurse. He and his wife had a son with severe disabilities who had been seen by many physicians.

Leila was having problems with keeping her balance. Mike told me about a medical specialist who had helped them limit their son's injuries from accidental falls. This physician was helpful, also, to Leila. Sometimes Mike and I would call each other just to talk and relax.

▶ *Look for "respite" allies*

Respite means getting a break from everyday routine and responsibilities. Some community organizations provide several hours of respite a week at no cost to people with demanding caregiving responsibilities. Some homecare agencies will provide respite companions for a reasonable fee. The expense is often worth it.

If I had not asked a local organization for help, we would not have met Marie. She spent an evening with Leila at least 40 weeks a year for seven years. We called her the Volunteer of the Century.

Respite goes both ways. Marie gave me a break and she gave Leila a break from me.

If there are no respite groups near you, your church or religious organization might find a volunteer for you. Maybe a neighbor will help you out.

▸ *Perhaps your employer can help*

Check on whether there are caregiver support groups where you work. If not, you might suggest starting one. Perhaps the human resources department also could assist employees such as you to find the services your parents need, including those who live at a distance.

Companies that develop employee assistance eldercare programs find that supporting these programs is an excellent investment. In 2006 the Metlife Mature Market Institute and the National Alliance for Caregivers published a study on the costs to businesses associated with the eldercare responsibilities of full-time employed caregivers. The estimated annual lost productivity cost to businesses nationwide: $33.6 billion.

The study found that these costs were associated with various factors, including absenteeism, work interruptions, emergencies and supervisory time devoted to overcoming these problems. Of course, constant employee stress also takes its toll on employee productivity.

Many companies provide some degree of eldercare employee assistance, primarily referrals to agencies that provide services such as homecare. Relatively few have established ambitious eldercare programs that substantially reduce employee caregiving-related problems. Some of the benefits offered by these businesses in addition to referrals: flexible work hours, job-sharing, employee seminars, one-on-one problem-solving help and subsidized emergency back-up assistance.

I have found that the best way to stay current on effective company eldercare programs is to search for "family-friendly companies." You will get several lists. Visit the web sites of several of these businesses and search for "eldercare." Usually you won't have to search the company's web site. You will find links to programs and benefits for caregiving employees on the company's home page.

▸ *Be open to finding allies among paid providers of services*

જી૪૭

Laura, one of Leila's more creative caregivers, came down the stairs clutching an assortment of brightly colored blouses and my mother's favorite necklaces. "Leila! It's time to start wearing your summer things. Let's see what you want to wear today, and then have coffee on the porch." Leila beamed. She had felt "low" when she awoke. Her body ached. Looking in her hand mirror made the start of the day even more difficult. "I can't believe what has happened to me. I don't like looking at myself anymore."

Within the hour, Leila was transformed. Laura helped her shower. Leila chose her aqua blouse, black slacks and her mother's pearl necklace. She put on her makeup, using that same hand mirror. Laura fixed her hair.

On the way to the porch, Laura had Leila look at herself in the front hall mirror. "Not bad, huh, Leila?" Leila smiled and told Laura she was "really something else." Then Leila had coffee and breakfast outdoors on a beautiful June morning as she chatted and laughed with one of her new best friends.

જી૪૭

Our closest allies were the women who helped Leila with her daily personal care needs, such as bathing and dressing. Laura was one of many aides who understood what motivated Leila and took advantage of it.

Leila's caregivers went out of their way to help me get respite time. Their help was priceless. I learned that even one caring and committed in-home worker can bring light and hope to your life. In Chapter 18 I discuss how to find reliable caregivers who will commit themselves to protecting your parents' best interests.

Several registered nurses (RNs) became invaluable allies. For instance, during a lengthy hospital stay, one of Leila's lungs collapsed. She needed a surgical procedure to get it functioning again. One of the RNs, Ruby, said to me: "The doctor to get for this is Dr. Brown. Don't have Dr. ___ do it. Marge, don't you think Dr. Brown is the best bet?" Marge agreed.

Leila's primary doctor arranged for Dr. Brown to do the procedure. Dr. Brown was expert and kind. I still marvel that these brave nurses dared to give me this advice. Nurses aren't supposed to share these kinds of opinions with patients or their families. These women, however, were invested in my mother's well-being and took a risk to help her get well again.

If you look for them, and are open to their help, you can find allies among other health and social service professionals, including physicians. There are examples of how to recruit these kinds of allies throughout this guide.

Leila Lynch celebrating a joyful occasion with two of her caregivers and good friends. (Late 1980s)

Our Unexpected Bonus: The Campaign

After the first couple of years with Leila, I had time to look around me at what she and I had going for us. We had more allies than I had realized. For instance, our pharmacists were also our friends. They always asked how Leila was doing and were very helpful to me.

A receptionist in our doctor's office helped me get through to busy nurses in urgent situations. The dietitian we met during one of Leila's several hospital stays told me to call her from our home whenever we needed her advice. These are only a few examples of the consideration we received from unexpected allies.

I realized that this was now more than just "taking care of Leila." We had a kind of campaign going for us. The "Let's Help Leila and Terry Do Well" campaign. Looking at our situation this way energized and relaxed me. I became more hopeful. We had a powerful force on our side: all our allies combined.

When I talked to Leila about the campaign, she smiled and told me it was wonderful to look at our lives this way. Our campaign members also liked seeing their contributions to our lives in this light.

CB80

Erik, a close friend, was stricken with a paralyzing illness at age 33, several years after Leila's death. He told me that the "campaign image" helped him through two frightening and difficult years in hospitals and nursing homes. "Many of my doctors, nurses and nurses' aides fought for my life. And then there were my family and friends and the people who brought me my meals. There were lots of others. I thought of all of you as a force that would fight along with me no matter what happened next."

Erik is now 40 and enjoys a productive and interesting life. The campaign continues to help him keep it that way.

CB80

In difficult times it can be hard to believe that anything remotely like a campaign can develop in your lives. Start with small steps. As you work with this guide, you may look up one day as I did and be pleasantly surprised.

Chapter 6

Your Life Is Important Too!

This chapter is directed at adult children who are under significant caregiving pressure, either short-or long-term. Even if you feel you do not fit this description, you may want to page through this chapter anyway in case it is more applicable to your life than you think it would be.

I *did* hit some straight!

03℘

Leila loved coming with me to my local golf range, which was surrounded by farm fields and oak trees. She'd sit in a favorite spot under one of those trees and chat with other onlookers while she watched me miss-hit ball after ball into the cornfield to the south. I would turn and wave at her after hitting a good one and she would wave back, encouraging me to do it again. At the end of my flawed self-improvement session, she would tell me the last few shots showed progress. We'd laugh and agree that we had to return soon.

℘03

Unless you take care of yourself from the time you start helping your parents, you are not likely to do as well as you can for them. You both will lose.

As my caregiving skills improved, I found time for recreation. I was fortunate. It was also lucky that some activities were those Leila could enjoy with me, such as going out to dinner, visiting friends and going to the golf range. We started to enjoy everyday life.

According to Leila and the women who helped us, I was less irritable and more fun to be around. My caregiving skills improved. I now understood the connection between doing well for myself and doing well by my mother.

There are many tips in this chapter. It may be unrealistic to try to follow them all. Don't be discouraged if you can't. When you are overwhelmed with tasks and worries, doing something just for you can seem unimaginable. Please try, anyway.

Some of the keys to reducing my anxiety may not work for you. Keep looking for the little things in life that make you feel better. You may be surprised at the difference they can make.

I learned that maintaining my physical health was essential to maintaining my emotional well-being, and vice-versa, and that treating them as two distinct goals was the most effective approach to stress reduction.

Take Care of Your Physical Self

Find a way to get regular exercise. It's an investment.

I found no better stress reducer than exercise. I forced myself to take walks, even in cold weather, and when I did almost every problem seemed less difficult. If you would prefer riding an exercise bike in front of the television set or while listening to music, do that. The key is to get your heart pumping, *as long as it's not contrary to your doctor's advice!* You will not regret it. There is plenty of research that ties exercise to improved mental and physical health.

For information on various ways to put exercise into a busy life and to ensure that exercise is safe for you, go to www.medlineplus.gov and search for *Exercise and physical fitness*.

Try to get enough sleep.

I know this can be hard to do. Whenever I got too little sleep, my anxiety increased. Sneak in a short nap during the day if you can.

Eat well.

Overloaded caregivers have notoriously poor diets. This is one reason they become ill. I could not afford to get sick and I worked at making sure Leila and I had a balanced diet. I did not have time to prepare meals from scratch very often. I "served" healthful frozen dinners and other meals that took little time. I supplemented them with salads, fruit and whole-grain bread. And cookies. We each had to have our cookies.

See a physician for regular physical checkups.

Protect Your Emotional Well-Being

Try to do these things for yourself.

▶ *Find someone to talk to.*
Look for someone who values you and understands what you are trying to do for your parent. In even the best parent-offspring caregiving situations some resentment and anger about your situation is normal. Feeling misunderstood or unappreciated by friends or other family members is common. Wondering just how much longer you will have to live like this is not something to be ashamed of.

I had several friends to whom I could express these feelings without having to hear: "Well, Terry, it may be time to think about moving your mother to…" They supported what I was doing for Leila and understood I needed to let these emotions out so they didn't take over my life.

▶ *Look for the positives.*
Being negative can become a way of life. Both you and your parent will be miserable because of it.

▶ *Find something to look forward to each day.*
This was one of the lessons my dad taught me when I was a child. He owned a shoe store and worked most of the time, so he had to make an effort to put fun in his life.

I followed my father's advice. For instance, I saved time each night for activities I enjoyed, after I helped Leila go to bed. Usually it was watching a movie or reading something that allowed me to escape. If it is nothing more than having a friend over for coffee but you look forward to it, schedule it and keep doing it. Talk about topics that distract you from your daily concerns, unless you need help solving a problem or need to vent your emotions.

▶ *Find a pleasant daily diversion.*
Start a hobby. Read mystery novels. Grow beautiful houseplants. Find something that absorbs you and gives you pleasure.

▶ *Try to take vacations, even brief ones.*
It was stressful for me to leave Leila, even for a day. I had to schedule aides, neighbors and respite volunteers so that she would have twenty-four hour care. I was fortunate that government programs covered some of the costs of this extra care.

In spite of my anxiety about leaving Leila, I got away for short visits to friends now and then. Also, my work took me away from home several days each month. It was always worth the stress of setting up these days away. They recharged my battery.

▶ *Get out of the house.*
For some of you, a "vacation" might be limited to short breaks. When it seems that your life mission is to do as much as you can as fast as you can, an hour of relaxation is a treasure. I found that even grocery shopping was a welcome break.

▶ *Have a helper take over some everyday tasks.*
Ideally this would be another family member or friend. I have a friend who spends some of most evenings at her parents' home after work. "Paying a neighbor to clean my house has made a big difference in how I feel."

▶ *Ask for help and accept it.*
"Really? Could you mow my lawn once in a while?" This is so important it is worth repeating.

▶ *Get help for depression.*
Clinical depression is one of the family caregiver's most dangerous enemies. You may be under so much stress that hopeless feelings, acute anxiety, constant sadness or other depression symptoms seem normal. These days, family physicians treat many patients for this illness. They know other professionals who are skilled at helping people with mental health disorders. (See Resource Appendix, page 248.)

▶ *Go easy on yourself.*
You are not going to please everyone, get everything done, do everything "right" or be a nice person all the time. Friends or family members may feel slighted because you have less time for them. It helped me to try to step outside our situation and look at it through a stranger's eyes. I was doing a lot for my mother. It was understandable that I sometimes would not handle it well.

▶ *Have compassion for your parent.*
Leila was easy to get along with but many times I was irritated by questions that seemed never to end. Her impaired memory made it impossible for Leila to keep track of our daily schedule. "Terry, are you going somewhere? When do you get back?" In my worst moments I would ask her how many times I had to tell her.

Compassion helped me avoid these demeaning comments most of the time. All the questions were irritating. But how must it feel to lose your mind, as Leila sometimes described the impact of her memory disorder? Looking at it this way made life easier on Leila and on her son.

▶ *Try to get organized…at least a little.*
Your reaction probably is *In the middle of all this I have to figure out how to be organized, too?* I hope you try. Reducing the *I'm so scattered!* aspect of caregiving can boost your morale. At first some of my anxiety was caused by trying to keep track of things and by those *I know I put it somewhere* moments. I felt less pressured as soon as I was better organized.

A Few Tips

✓ Keep it simple. And don't rely on your memory.

✓ Use an appointment book. Mine had plenty of space for each day's schedule. It had a pocket for papers I needed with me, and a large notepad which I used for to-do lists, questions for my mother's doctors, and for general management of our daily life.

✓ Ask your pharmacist to help you manage your parent's medication schedule.

✓ Use an in-box for bills and other important paperwork and an out-box for papers that need filing. Throw out anything you are unlikely to need. My motto: *Less clutter, less anxiety.*

✓ Have a small filing cabinet for records you should keep. I limited the file folders to important areas such as: insurance; income taxes; financial matters; Leila's medical records and bills; ideas on people and services to help us; and articles on golf. I paid a high school student for an hour of filing each week.

✓ Take time to consider what comes first. When I went on errands I planned my "trip" to limit the *Oh, no! I have to go back to the drug store for ___* experiences.

✓ Help your parent get organized, too. We put important items on a large daily calendar that was always at Leila's side. We kept her makeup and other personal items in the same place to reduce her confusion.

✓ Organize only what you need to. Caregiving provides an excuse for not worrying about the trivial. I used that excuse a lot, for instance when clothes didn't make it from the laundry basket to my dresser drawers.

If you have a well-organized ally who offers to help, *please* just say "Yes!" If she doesn't think of it, she may be happy to help, if you ask.

▶ *How about a furry friend?*
If you spend a good deal of time alone with your parent, consider adding a pet to your household. During the last few years with Leila, we shared our home with a tough and affectionate one-eyed cat who appeared at our door one winter night. He brightened our world even in the worst of times.

▶ *Celebrate the victories.*
At first, whenever Leila made it through another hospital stay, or survived some other crisis, I immediately started worrying about *What is going to go wrong next?* When I realized how damaging this was to my mental health, I worked hard to change to *How wonderful it is to have made it through this crisis. We are so lucky to still be together.*

I held small parties in Leila's hospital room on the nights before she was discharged. Some of the nurses and their aides would stop in and we would thank them for their help. Each January, I gave a birthday party for Leila. Our guests were our neighbors and the women who helped us. Some brought their young children.

These moments were wonderful affirmations of the good that had come along with the difficult times. We were celebrating the success of our campaign to help Leila Lynch live contentedly in her home.

Fight the bad habits.

▶ *Try not to let guilt control you.*

കൃഞ

I taught a short course for family caregivers at a community college. I called it "Helping Aging Parents and Yourselves: Keys to Coping with Family Overload." Class enrollment was higher than expected. I asked what in the course description attracted them.—"Overload!"

Much of that collective overload came from guilt. Guilt about leaving a parent with another caregiver so a daughter could have time for herself. About not doing a better job of caregiving. About not spending more time with their own families. As one woman talked about the demands her mother was making on her, a classmate blurted out, "Just say no!" There was sympathetic laughter around the room.

ക്കൃഞ

How far should you go to accommodate your parent's wishes? No one else can tell you. Some dedicated and overwhelmed sons and daughters mistakenly let guilt dictate these decisions. They might have a parent move in with them because of guilt, not because it is the best thing to do for either party.

Guilt tells caregivers not to take breaks or ask for help. They don't want to admit they need to get away from their parent and the stress of caregiving. They might feel they are letting their parent down if they employ someone to help with bathing or other personal care needs.

Sometimes a parent contributes to these feelings by becoming upset if the daughter or son even hints at bringing in extra help or taking a vacation. *I didn't realize I was such a burden* can cause the caregiver's resentment to build and feeds her anxiety. Caregiver illnesses and abusive behavior toward the dependent parent are two potential destructive outcomes of these situations.

▶ *Avoid "No one can do this right except me".*
This leads quickly to caregiver martyrdom: *I have no life. Don't bother worrying about me.* If the only people I left my mother with were those who did everything just the way I did, I seldom would have made it past our front porch. If they were careful about her safety, medications, meals, exercise and mental health, it was OK if they made her bed differently than I would have or didn't clean the kitchen up to my (minimal) standards.

▶ *Don't let the details get to you.*

CRED

A caregiver who was in our home for the first time told me, "I know about you. You are the man who leaves all the notes." I laughed along with her. I knew my reputation among the women who worked for us.

CRED

I attended to detail constantly. How could it have been otherwise? Leila had several medications that had to be given at the right time. I, and "her girls" (the women who helped her) had to stay on the lookout for signs of heart failure, low sodium and potassium, bladder infections and other serious medical problems. If we left Leila's walker beyond her reach, she might risk falling in order to get to it instead of calling for help.

It was details like these that made up the "notes" I left for our aides. These notes were useful not only for guiding these women through the day, but also for informing them on what had been done prior to their shift. And each caregiver left notes for the other aides who followed them.

I, however, became obsessed with detail. Until I identified what was not important, I was more anxious than I needed to be. I was unreasonably demanding on the women who helped us. Reminding them to help Leila exercise was essential. Having them do it at the same time each day was not.

Being careful is one of the traits of the successful caregiver. Watch out for going too far. My mother and her aides eventually straightened me out. The lesson was: Identify those things that must be done precisely and at a certain time in order to ensure Leila's health and well-being. Don't worry about the rest of it.

▶ *Don't obsess over what you can't change.*
You are doing so much for your mother, yet your siblings never express their gratitude. Your father never thanks you. Your husband does not cook for your children the same way you do. Try to let these things go. You do not have excess energy to spend on situations or attitudes you are not going to change. Staying upset over them will only make you less productive and discharge your battery even further.

▶ *Don't try to deal with everything at once.*
It will fry your brain and reduce your effectiveness.

Remember a Certain Caregiver's Confessions

A university professor asked me to talk to her social work class. The topic: "How to be an effective advocate for a family member." I told her I would be happy to. Before she hung up, she added that it would be interesting to learn how my life as Leila's caregiver and advocate affected my daily life.

At first, I was full of myself and what I could teach the class about looking out for a loved one's best interests. Then I remembered: The professor wanted to know how this experience was affecting me. To do well by the students I would have to look at myself and be open about what I had found.

As I thought about *"What I am like now"* my presentation title changed from something flattering to: "A Caregiver's Confessions." My talk did focus on strategies for helping Leila get good medical care and other kinds of services. But I admitted to the class that my day-to-day tasks, although rewarding, were fueling some personality traits I would not want on my resume. The presentation outline I used in this class included

I (hesitantly) admit I am

▸ Anxious

▸ Too often irritable

▸ Obsessed with detail

▸ Overwhelmed and often insecure

▸ Sometimes worried about how much longer I would be living like this . . . and sometimes feeling guilty for worrying about it.

Does this list sound familiar? I learned most of the advice I include in this chapter the hard way. I also found I rarely could do it all. Sometimes I felt it was all hopeless.

"I am tough? Really?"

᯾

Leila was in the hospital and sicker than I had realized. I was overwhelmed. Although I had helped Leila through several crises, this time it seemed too much to handle. I called Lynn, a close friend, and told him of my desperation.

He told me he always had been impressed with my toughness, my capacity for getting Leila through difficult times. My response was "Really?" Lynn reminded me that I knew Leila better than anyone else did. I should

trust my instincts and not let the overpowering hospital environment shake my confidence. And I could always call on him and other friends for help.

It was the boost I needed. I went back to Leila's hospital room, sat down next to her bed, and made my plan for helping her through the first day of another hospitalization.

☙❧

Helping Your Parents Long Distance

Chapter 7

Getting a Jump on Trouble

Put Prevention at the Top of Your List

My long-distance caregiving began several years before Leila and I became housemates. I spent time with her in Wisconsin after she fractured her hip. Then she lived with me in Washington until she was ready to be on her own. Another time, Leila broke her wrist while visiting me. After seeing her through surgery and rehabilitation, I went home with her for a brief stay.

Those experiences should have been my wake-up calls. Unfortunately, they weren't. I didn't recognize that an active and vital woman was teetering on the brink of dependency and that I needed to do something about it. I didn't know then how much difference I might have made.

Problem prevention is important in every situation. It is extraordinarily important when families are miles apart. Here are a few things I didn't do that can help protect your parents' self-reliance:

Plan some prevention visits to your parents

Some assistance when nothing is wrong beats a lot of long-distance emergency attention later.

Convincing your parents you will not abandon them in difficult times is a key to frank discussions about maintaining their quality of life (Chapter 3). It is difficult to have these very personal conversations on the telephone. Also, their distance from you may increase your parents' reluctance to have these discussions under any circumstances. "If something goes wrong, the nursing home might be all that I have." Leila was less open about her medical problems because of this sense of isolation.

I don't want to be a burden is magnified by distance. Leila might have brought up her fainting spells if I lived near her. She didn't want me to worry about this problem from almost 1,000 miles away.

If I could do it over again, I would try to ease Leila's fears and erase the communications barrier between us in casual discussions at her kitchen table while she was active and self-reliant. Unfortunately, we did not have that conversation until Leila's health problems hit me between the eyes.

Leila Lynch at age 30 on the family farm, with friend.

Once you can have a conversation that is not colored by anxiety, get an idea of what your parents "really want" from the rest of their lives. Do they wish to hang onto their home even if life gets difficult? Does living in an apartment somewhere down the line seem attractive? Might they be interested in that now? I would not have this kind of discussion until you have read each chapter in "Determining and Safeguarding 'What's Best.'"

Also, to learn more about getting to the heart of what your parents might prefer in the long run, I suggest you read Edna's story in Chapter 21, "Edna: Almost, but Not Quite." Remember to weave a discussion of this guide, at least the Eight Rules, into your conversations.

Emphasizing long-distance prevention does not mean smothering your parents with anxious attention. Communicate as well as possible with them, be on guard for preventable problems, and get involved as soon as they need your help.

▶ *Although my emphasis is on what you can do when you visit your parents, use whatever methods are most practical in your circumstances.*

Nurture relationships with allies

Leila lived most of her adult life in Racine, where I grew up. I knew the quality of local hospitals and the reputations of many physicians. I was acquainted with her neighbors, friends, and members of her church. It was relatively easy to find emergency assistance for her, even from long distance.

If your parent lives somewhere unfamiliar to you, you have more to do. Meet her neighbors. If she doesn't know anyone who lives nearby, be her ambassador. Ask her about her closest friends. Who would go out of their way for her? Take her and her friends to dinner.

Pick up your parent's prescriptions and take time to chat with the pharmacists. If your father is having some health problems, arrange to go with him to his primary physician. Be creative.

Prevent accidents waiting to happen

Injuries from falls, often hip fractures, rank near the top of the causes of elders' hospitalizations and admissions to nursing homes. Falls are a leading cause of death from injuries among our older population.

▣ *Remember, difficulty with keeping one's balance should be approached as a medical problem, not as a normal part of aging.*

See Chapter 2, page 9, for more detail on how to prevent falls. Other harmful and deadly accidents that occur at home are also preventable. I discuss home safety at greater length in Chapter 19.

Be ready for emergencies

On visits to your parents, and with some advance long-distance telephone networking, find out

▶ who to call spur-of-the moment to connect you to various kinds of community services;

▶ which medical specialists, such as surgeons, have the best reputations.

Consider organizing your parents' friends

Friends and neighbors often come to the aid of an ill or injured older person. Why not try to convince your parents and a few friends to help each other to *prevent* these problems? If they share responsibility for learning about disease and accident prevention, and help each other head off problems, they may avoid some distressing hospital and nursing home visits.

Stay in touch

Communicating regularly with your parents, but not overdoing it, helps maintain an open and trusting relationship. It improves your chances of hearing remarks such as *By the way dear, there is something I wanted to ask you.* Do not put your parents through an inquisition each time you talk. "Prevention" can come to mean *How can we prevent the kids from calling us so much?*

Consider using electronic mail, as well as the telephone. E-mail saves time and money, yet keeps you connected. People are sometimes more likely to share personal information in writing rather than over the telephone.

Technology is constantly expanding e-mail options. I have an older friend who finds "Web TV" easy to use. (Call the TV service provider.) Public libraries provide no-cost e-mail services. So do some community-health libraries. (Resource Appendix, page 250.)

If getting out to these places is difficult for your parent and he cannot or will not pay for e-mail services, paying for them yourself can be a worthwhile prevention expense.

Snoop if you must

Do this only when you are worried about a parent's health and are not getting what you need to know. It means: Check with other family members or your father's friends and neighbors to see how he is doing. He rightfully might see this as a violation of his privacy and dignity. However, it could save him from injury or even death. If I had followed my own advice, I would have learned much sooner that a neighbor ". . . had been concerned about Leila for some time."

Be Prepared for Long-Distance Emergencies

From emergency to long-term solution

⋯

Judy called me long distance. She had been up all night after traveling to be with her mother in the hospital. Her mother had been injured in a fall at home. She was disoriented and confused. Hospital physicians found that poor nutrition was at the root of these problems. Judy wanted advice on nursing homes. Her mother would be ready for discharge within a couple of days. I suggested that we try to come up with a better plan.

Our solution: Work with the hospital dietitian on a diet for her mother to follow at home, set up in-home assistance several times a week, and have a favorite neighbor check on whether her mother was eating properly. This solution worked well. It got even better when Judy's brother decided to move in with their mother. She lived at home for the rest of her life, which was several more years.

⋙⋘

▶ If an emergency situation calls for you to travel to your parent, and you can, go when you will be most needed. Getting to her mother's side right away was Judy's key to getting her back home. Be sure an alternate healthcare agent will be involved while you are traveling. (See page 41.)

▶ Recognize that you will be under even more stress than you would be if you lived near your parent. You might believe the only choice is to work out a solution hastily, as Judy was tempted to do. These kinds of "solutions" often turn out poorly.

Sometimes you will be most useful at first on the telephone. For instance, you may not want to be traveling when your parent needs your help with a decision on whether she should have immediate surgery. Check on whether your parent's medical files, including hospital records, contain her advance directive and medical information release form.

Whatever the crisis, your first step might be to arrange short-term assistance from your parents' allies, a home healthcare agency or a geriatric-care manager, whose services are described later in this chapter. You can work out more permanent and perhaps less costly arrangements later.

The federal Family and Medical Leave Act requires many employers to provide eligible employees with up to 12 workweeks of unpaid leave to care for parents and other immediate family members who have serious medical problems. Some employers pay for medical and caregiving leave.

Frontload when you can

To enable Leila to recover at home from injuries such as her pelvic fractures

- ▶ I decided that investing considerable time in her recovery, first in the hospital, then at home, was best for both of us.

- ▶ We spent a lot of money for a limited time on in-home help.

I call this the Frontload Principle: To spend less time and money later, you will sometimes have to spend more time and money now.

⊡ *To frontload, you may have to disrupt your lives in the short run. You may have to manage chaos. Ultimately, it can ensure that your parents' lives and yours are better and less chaotic than they otherwise would have been.*

Lucky I called

☙❧

Aunt Ethel had been admitted to a western Wisconsin nursing home. I called to check on her from Washington. I told the nurse that Aunt Ethel's heart medication had once been left off her medical chart while she was hospitalized. I wanted to be sure that hadn't happened again. (Today, the nurse would not have been authorized to talk to me about my aunt's illness without her written consent.)

The nurse put me on hold while she checked Aunt Ethel's medical records. She was flustered when she returned to the telephone. No heart medication this time, either. The nurse had this error corrected within the hour.

☙❧

While I was still living in Washington, I could not always be with Leila when she was hospitalized. I helped guide her care over the telephone through daily calls to nurses, physical therapists, physicians' offices, neighbors and a sister who was with her much of the time. If Leila had been in a nursing home for rehabilitation, I would have used the same approach.

It Can Work: Long-Term Care from a Distance

Be there or work with others to set up the service plan

Your mother is receiving post-surgery rehabilitation therapy in a nursing home. Soon she will be ready to go back home, but she will be less capable of getting along on her own, at least for a while.

Ideally, you would spend some time with your mother to help put together the services she needs. If you cannot do that, you might be able to work long distance with an ally. As Judy did, you might find someone in your mother's life to help monitor and coordinate her care. A volunteer visitor, paid companion or independent nurse's aide might take on the coordinator's role.

Another option: Work with a geriatric-care manager. These professionals are expert in assessing an elder's health status and home situation and in setting up the help their clients need. Many can provide long-term services. Their services can be costly, but these care managers may assist your parent to save money in the long run by helping her avoid a nursing home.

Be prepared for the next steps

If it becomes hazardous for your parent to live on her own without constant in-home assistance, perhaps a provider of live-in services might be the answer. (Key Resources, page 248.) If creative arrangements won't work, unless your parent has substantial financial resources it will be difficult to enable her to continue to live in her home. The cost will be too great. Alternative residences may be the next best choice.

Before you suggest that your parents move, be sure you have read "Helping Your Parents Remain at Home."

▣ *Pay attention to the well-being of a parent who is caring for a spouse. Use what you learn in this guide to assist him to get as much support as possible. Be sure he gets some breaks. Watch for signs of extreme stress, exhaustion, depression or other illnesses. This guide will assist you to work with him on your mother's medical issues.*

Heading Off
and Tackling
Medical Problems

Chapter 8

Common Sense Works

You don't need a completely new way of dealing with problems when you enter the world of *what to do about Mom and Dad*. Common sense works well. This chapter describes steps that can help you and your parents manage, and even prevent, many health-related problems that threaten quality of life.

Don't feel guilty or inadequate because you can't use each step every time. You may be under too much pressure or events may be moving too fast. I learned these steps by trial and error over many years. Try to stick to them, but don't beat yourself up when you cannot.

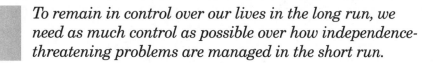

To remain in control over our lives in the long run, we need as much control as possible over how independence-threatening problems are managed in the short run.

Step 1: Start at the Beginning—Try to Remedy Problems That May Seem Unavoidable or Natural

Don't assume your parents' most difficult problems cannot be remedied without first helping them search for the root causes. Look beyond "old" for a more specific explanation. For instance, if your mother is confused, or has balance problems, find out why before you decide the answer is "someplace safer." The problem at the root of her difficulties may be correctable.

Several times in Leila's last years she abruptly became more confused. She was fortunate to have a physician who searched for the root causes. Each time, he found Leila's problems were related to a decrease in her blood pressure, not to an increase in her age. A change in her fluid intake solved the problem every time.

Some root causes, such as Alzheimer's disease, cannot be remedied. But even the impact of this nightmarish disease can sometimes be reduced for a while if you start at the beginning.

Larry had asked me for help regarding his father's situation (Chapter 5). They lived far apart and his father was having fainting episodes. He also had developed some problems with short-term memory and his hearing. Larry also was worried about other, lesser problems. After sorting through these concerns, we agreed to focus on his father's health problems first.

> ▶ *What were the urgent problems?*
> Children may have to deal with immediate threats to life and well-being before, or while, they look for causes. Larry's most urgent problem: Protecting his father from serious injuries that might result from his fainting episodes.

> ▶ *What were the roots of his father's fainting and forgetfulness?*
> I agreed to help Larry look for them.

Before our meeting ended I took Larry back to two problems we had set aside. He was upset by dust in his father's home. I asked him if his father would accept a cleaning service if Larry would pay for it. He thought it was likely. He was concerned that his father might start a fire by forgetting food on the stove. Did his father have a microwave oven? "No." Would he cook with one if he had one? "Probably."

CXEXO

I helped Larry find a geriatric clinic near his father. Geriatric physicians specialize in medical care for older people. Larry and I found in-home workers and respite volunteers who could spend time with his father to reduce the risk of a fainting injury. Larry could relax somewhat until he could get away from work and help his dad discover the causes of his medical problems.

Larry called me a month later. He had taken his father to the clinic. Its physicians discovered that one of his father's prescriptions was causing his fainting episodes and confusion. Since changing medications, his father was doing much better. But he wasn't ready to talk about hearing aids. Larry decided he would work on that concern the next time he visited his dad.

CXEXO

Step 2: Find the Best Medical Care You Can

CXEXO

"It's Alzheimer's." Leila's physician dropped this bomb while Leila waited in the examining room. I was uncomfortable with the diagnosis. Leila had been given only a physical examination. I called the Alzheimer's Association in Milwaukee. They suggested a second opinion and recommended several geriatric clinics.

Additional testing at one of these clinics indicated that Leila probably did not have Alzheimer's disease. They believed her memory loss and confusion were caused by small blood clots in her brain. The doctor prescribed medication to prevent further clotting. It wasn't a cure, but Leila's confusion did not worsen. Getting a second opinion from an excellent physician had preserved the quality of Leila's life and saved us each from avoidable anguish.

CR℘

To get to the roots of your parent's health problems your parent's physician should be skilled at geriatric medicine. Many family doctors, internists and medical specialists, such as cardiologists, understand geriatric medicine well. Often, your parents' primary physician will do just fine when you apply what you learn in this guide. Sometimes it may be best to seek out a new physician who specializes in geriatrics.

How do you locate expert physicians?

If your parent is not satisfied with his current physician, does not have a doctor, or needs one trained in geriatric medicine:

> ▸ *Try networking.*
> This was the most useful method for me. Networking is the process you use when you ask someone if he knows a good auto mechanic or day-care provider or house painter. It works for healthcare, too.
>
> Who might be able to help you find the right doctor? I always began with hospital or home-health nurses. These nurses usually know the reputations of a community's doctors. So do pharmacists. These professionals will have to be certain you will keep your information source confidential before sharing anything negative. Check with members of the clergy. Contact the Key Resources, page 248.
>
> If someone cannot help you directly, always ask: "Do you know anyone who might have ideas for us?" Contact national, state, or local organizations that provide information and advice on health conditions common to older persons. They will tell you where you can find specialists in the medical problems that concern you. These

organizations usually will not recommend specific physicians or clinics, but they might if you ask. (Resource Appendix, page 251.)

If your parent has an excellent physician, there should be less need to network when you are seeking additional specialized care. I learned that these physicians generally collaborate primarily with other excellent physicians.

Sometimes primary doctors regularly refer (send) patients to other physicians who work in the same medical clinic. You may need to ask for a referral to a physician who works elsewhere, but some specialists do not require referrals. Original Medicare does not limit patients to a certain group of physicians. If your parent is in a private Medicare Advantage plan, there might be limitations. (See page 17.)

▶ *Go to geriatric clinics.*
It can be worth traveling some distance to these clinics, which often are associated with medical schools and hospitals. I took Leila 40 miles to geriatric clinics in Milwaukee several times. It was always worth the trip.

▶ *Contact physician specialists who teach at medical schools.*
These doctors are likely to have advanced knowledge about the illnesses in which they specialize.

Several web sites enable you to check on the credentials of physicians and surgeons and find board certified physicians. Board certified doctors have received training beyond medical school and have certificates showing they passed demanding examinations in their medical specialty. (Resource Appendix, page 262.)

Some physicians choose to not participate in the Medicare program or the Medicaid program (page 45). Some who do participate may charge higher fees than some other physicians. (See the Medicare discussion, page 13.)

Step 3: Help the Doctors Diagnose the Problems

Fill in the blanks

If your parent is unlikely or unable to provide specifics about her medical problems, do not assume the physician will think of everything. You and your parent have personal information that can be essential to a diagnosis. Doctors are human. They can make mistakes. They can miss something.

If you cannot accompany your parent on visits to her physician, perhaps one of her friends or neighbors might go with her. Develop a checklist of questions and important personal information for that person to refer to. Your parent will have to sign a consent form giving the doctor permission to speak with that person about your parent's medical condition (page 43).

Another option: Set up a telephone conversation between you and the physician or one of the nurses who assists him.

Do your homework

Taking an hour to learn about possible causes of a medical condition can be the key to an accurate diagnosis. I am not talking about becoming an instant medical expert. Learn enough to ask useful questions and assist the doctor to think about why something may be happening. Quality physicians welcome input and speculation from informed patients and family.

Finding out how Alzheimer's disease is properly diagnosed changed my mother's life, and mine. How hard was it to find out about testing for Alzheimer's disease? I had to call the Alzheimer's Association of Southeastern Wisconsin (this was 1985) and talk to one of their staff. It took me an hour. How long would it take to get this information today? If you have Internet access, you can cut that time in half.

You will find help with researching medical problems at community-health libraries at www.medlineplus.gov. Click on *Other Resources*, then

Libraries. Various reputable web sites can direct you to medical schools and clinics in the forefront of research and treatment of difficult medical conditions. (Resource Appendix, page 251.)

For financial assistance that may be available for people with specific medical problems, search www.medlineplus.gov for *Financial assistance*. Be sure to see the Resource Appendix, page 251, for comprehensive information resources related to health care.

Step 4: Learn About Appropriate Treatments

The more I understood about options for treating Leila's medical conditions, the better her health became. It helped me ask good questions and make useful suggestions.

Physicians sometimes don't find out right away about advances in the treatment of various diseases. Doing some research may teach you something your doctor does not yet know. For instance: A friend sent me an article on a new treatment for osteoporosis. I told my mother's doctor about it. He checked it out with a colleague and started Leila on a medication that increased her bone strength and reduced her pain.

The diagnostic information resources discussed in Step 3 will have treatment-related information, as well.

▣ *Help your parent understand his treatment options and make the best decisions consistent with his wishes.*

Step 5: Double-Check Diagnoses and Treatments

If a medical problem is not improving or if you are uncomfortable with the original diagnosis, ask your doctor to refer you to a physician who specializes in this health condition. If a risky treatment procedure is recommended, such as major surgery, seeing another physician before proceeding is usually a good idea.

Don't let loyalty to a physician cloud your judgment. Medicare pays for second opinions. The best doctors seek help from other physicians when they are uncertain about diagnoses or treatment. If this approach is not productive, network your way to another physician yourself.

Your parent may be uncomfortable with seeking a second opinion out of loyalty to his doctor. If you tell him about the Eight Rules he might be more likely to follow your advice. I found that *Please do this for me, Mom* sometimes worked. *I know what is best, Mom* never did.

Technology is assisting medical professionals to diagnose and treat health problems from a distance. The terms for the practice of medicine with technologies such as computers, electronic mail and long-distance health monitoring devices are "telehealth" and "telemedicine." This technology should eventually be helpful to people in rural areas, others who have difficulty getting to doctors' offices and those who need constant health monitoring.

Chapter 9

Making Things Happen

You have sorted the problems. You know what problem-solving steps you should take but don't know how to put them into action. Your mother likes her new doctor, who is very busy. Not much time for conversation or for working with her patients' family members. How do you get your parent's doctor(s) to slow down and listen to questions and suggestions? How do you get these physicians to go out of their way to give your parent the best possible care?

We all should have physicians like this

ॐ

Dr. Jones called me into his office, while Leila and his nurse chatted in the exam room. Leila had been living with me in Washington for a while. Dr. Jones was an excellent physician who had established a comfortable and supportive relationship with us. This was our last office visit. We were returning to Wisconsin. The doctor closed his door and said, "I'm going to miss you guys—especially your mother."

I asked him if he was going to miss her, or was it really the chocolate chip cookies she baked for him. He laughed and admitted it was hard to see the cookies go.

Then Dr. Jones said, "Knowing Leila has changed the way I practice medicine. Before I met her, I provided good care to my older patients. However, I realize now that, because of the chronic health problems of many of them, I believed I could not do much to affect the quality of their lives. But your mother still sees herself as a young woman. Her days are as precious to her, in spite of her pain, as they ever were. Because of your mom I will never look at an older person the same way again."

As we left Dr. Jones' office, he said "One more thing. Get the new doc trained, and then step back, as you did with me."

CR8O

Dr. Jones was one of the finest people, and best doctors, we ever encountered. However, before he met my mother, his treatment decisions were affected by the "labels" he associated with his older patients. For him, "frail," "disabled" and "old" added up to limited quality of life. Leila's spirit and enjoyment of life, in spite of her painful medical problems, helped him see beyond her age and frailty. He observed, listened, reconsidered and improved his practice of medicine. We never forgot him.

I realized later that I had used several strategies to assist Leila to open Dr. Jones' eyes. This chapter describes those strategies and what else I did to "train" Dr. Jones and the doctors that followed to work with us as partners. I don't mean to imply that all our physicians needed this training. Nevertheless, these tactics helped in even the best situations.

Strategies that Improved Leila's Care and Quality of Life

CR80

I mentioned to Leila's new physician in Wisconsin the importance of screening her for uterine cancer. The doctor's reply: "You want the whole ball of wax? Sometimes it is better not to know." I told him my mother wanted the same healthcare and choices that his younger patients had.

CR80

Set high expectations

Make clear you don't want your parent to receive second-class medical care. Usually, your actions will say this for you. But do not hesitate to say it directly.

Talk to the physician as though she is an ally

—even if she has not yet become one. "Your suggestions during our last visit improved my mother's appetite a lot. I really appreciate your figuring that out with us."

Model the behavior you want to see in others

Don't treat your parent as a "baby" or with disrespect. Others need to see that *you* value your parent.

Make clear the customer is not you

If your father's physician directs questions to you instead of to him, you might say, "Let's ask my father about that." Even if your parent has impaired memory, help him to communicate directly with the doctor.

Help your parent tell her story

Your mother might not have a pleasant personality. She may not be likeable. She may have dementia and be unable to connect with her doctor. You may have to do more to draw others to her than I had to do for Leila. I noticed that just telling Leila's doctors she was a great baker or an outstanding teacher could make a difference in how they viewed her.

Connect with the insiders

Establish friendly relationships with the doctor's nurses and with staff at the reception desk. Nurses are the front-line advocates for patients and their family members. Nurses and reception staff are excellent communication links to the doctors.

If the doctor's staff includes a physician's assistant (PA) or nurse practitioner (NP), don't assume you must always see or talk with the doctor. PAs and NPs are well-trained in many aspects of healthcare. They usually are able to spend more time with patients than physicians can. And they can go directly to the doctor with a concern that comes up during your office visit.

Remember, you are not the only one under pressure. Most physicians, nurses and other service providers have large work loads. Just as you should not be shy, you should avoid being too demanding. Don't expect a nurse who is jumping from room to room to answer a question that can wait. Learn to choose the right time. Ultimately, you will get more information, and action, if you do.

Don't be shy

Physicians are on the move from patient to patient. We often are reluctant to ask them questions. And making suggestions? It can be hard even to form the words. Nevertheless, the medical care your parent receives will improve and your anxieties will lessen when you come out of your shell. It takes practice. Once you have done it, it will be easier the next time. If you are hesitant, think about what's at stake: Your parent's life. No physician ever said "not now" when I asked him to answer a few more questions, even when he was walking out the door.

Be organized and to the point. Have a list of questions to ask and information to share. Try to personalize the visit (*How are your children?*) without talking too much. You want the physician to still be in the room when you get to the list.

Be respectful and tactful

Anything that sounds like an accusation will push the physician or other medical staff away. It is the opposite of what you should do to draw them into a partnership. *My father is just as important as any other patient* is not nearly as effective as *Why do you think he still is in pain?*

Treat physicians and their staff the way you want your parent treated

I worked at being friendly to everyone who provided my mother a service. I also had a "secret weapon": Leila Lynch. She was interested in others' lives. When she asked doctors or nurses about their families, for instance, their manner often became more personal. I learned from Leila and followed her example.

Express gratitude

Although medical professionals provide services for which they are being paid, thank them. If their help means a lot to you, make sure they know it. One of Leila's home-health nurses told us that Leila was the only one of her patients who expressed appreciation for the quality of her work.

Be more assertive when you have no choice

Sometimes you have to draw the line. Showing your less pleasant side may be the only way to get something to happen or to get a point across. Don't make your comments personal and don't blow up, unless you cannot help it. Sometimes you may not be able to keep your cool.

Chapter 10

Illustrations: Deciding What Is Best in Difficult Situations

I try throughout this guide to help families decide how to make the best of life as loved ones age. I hope this chapter provides additional assistance with difficult decisions related to preserving the best interests of your parent while doing the right thing for yourself. It is not meant to instruct you on what is absolutely right or wrong in any circumstance.

What is Best Depends on What Your Parent Values Most

ॐ

Mark called to tell me his dad was in the hospital. His father, Roy, had a bulging aorta (an artery) in his abdomen. The physician believed Roy's artery could burst unless he had surgery. Mark didn't think his father was strong enough to survive the operation. "What should I do, Terry? Should I tell my dad's doctors surgery is out of the question?" I asked if his dad was still alert and thinking clearly. He said he was. I told Mark that as long as Roy was able to understand his options, he was the one to make that decision. Mark's responsibility was to help his dad think through his choices. Mark was relieved.

105

Mark and his father met with the doctor the next day. The doctor told Roy he had a reasonable chance of surviving the surgery, but the risk was higher than it would be for a person who was less frail. If he didn't have surgery, he would not be at immediate risk of death but would have to modify his daily life. Roy would have to be careful not to do something to cause the artery to rupture. At some point it might burst no matter how careful he was.

Roy decided to have the surgery. As Mark had feared, the surgical procedure proved too much for his father. Roy no longer had the strength to remain on his own. He spent his last year in a nursing home. Mark visited him frequently. He told me his dad never second-guessed his decision.

CRSO

Roy made the choice that gave him the best chance of living as he wished to. He did not want a life of constant concern about whether his aorta was about to burst. The doctor had been clear about the risks of surgery. Roy made an informed choice based on this information and his values about how he wanted to live the rest of his life. He was less concerned than Mark was about whether he would survive the surgery.

Did Mark act in his father's best interest?

We have a legal right to make decisions for ourselves, unless we are no longer capable of making them. That means we have the right to take the kind of risk Roy did. Mark understood this. In spite of the sad outcome, he was comfortable with the choice his father had made and about how he had helped him make it.

What if Roy had been too confused to understand his choices?

If Roy's reasoning capacity had been impaired temporarily—for instance by medication side effects—no immediate decision would have been necessary. Mark and his doctors could have waited until Roy was again capable of thinking for himself.

What if Roy's reasoning ability had been impaired permanently?

A healthcare power of attorney might have guided the doctors and his son in this situation. For instance, if Roy's confusion was caused by Alzheimer's disease and his directive was to avoid major surgery in the case of terminal illness, Mark's decision would have been relatively "clear."

If Roy had been permanently unable to understand complicated choices, but did not have a fatal illness, making the "right decision" would have been more difficult. Mark would have had to consider: "What would my dad do, now that he is facing a real-life crisis? Would he stick to what he decided two years ago when we were discussing what might happen?"

०३४०

Remaining as self-reliant as she could was one of Leila's foremost priorities. She knew that, at times, we would have to "push her" to help her stay as strong and mobile as possible. Her aides and I had to walk a fine line. Pushing her when she was tired or not feeling well would have been cruel. It was obvious that we should lighten up.

The rest of the time was tricky. We tried always to be careful about how we went about motivating Leila to walk. The rule was: Respect Leila and don't nag her. Get her to walk, anyway. "Come on, Leila, Terry will get mad at me if we don't walk down the block." "Leila, let's go out to the back yard to see the flowers." "Hey Mom, want to go to the post office with me?" We used many strategies that worked for many years.

०३४०

To Protect Best Interest: Resolve Family Conflicts

ଓଃ୫ଠ

Lucy's grandmother had several health conditions that required medication. She had stopped taking her pills because she believed they weren't doing her any good. Lucy's uncle, with whom her grandmother lived, believed it was his mother's right to stop these medications. Her grandmother was hospitalized for emergency care, too disoriented to understand what was happening.

Lucy's uncle and father had a long history of disagreeing with each other on "just about everything." It was no surprise that they disagreed over their mother's medical treatment. Her uncle held healthcare power of attorney and wasn't going to be swayed by his brother's opinion.

Lucy was able to get her dad and uncle to see that they couldn't focus on their mother's best interest because of their difficult relationship. Her father backed out of the discussions. Lucy helped her uncle determine the best course of medical care until her grandmother was again able to make decisions for herself.

Once her head was clear, and after a discussion with her physician, Lucy's grandmother agreed she would not discontinue any of her medications without first consulting him.

ଓଃ୫ଠ

You May Need to Find Your Mutual Best Interest

ଓଃ୫ଠ

Elaine's mother, June, was diagnosed with Alzheimer's disease by doctors at an excellent geriatric clinic. June lived alone in a lovely, large old home that was dear to her. Elaine lived several hundred miles away. She asked her mother to move to an apartment near her. June wanted to remain in her community and she wasn't happy about the thought of leaving her home. They worked out a compromise.

June agreed to move to an assisted living apartment in her home community, where she could get help as her illness progressed. Elaine would take responsibility for selling her home and use vacation time to help June move. Elaine also would work long distance with the staff of the assisted living residence on any problems that might arise and she would visit at least every few months.

This arrangement worked well for both women. June was in a place where she was content, near her friends, and safe. Ultimately, June moved to a nursing home associated with the assisted living residence, where she spent her last few years. Elaine continued her visits and her long-distance care.

CR80

The story of Elaine and June reminds us:

▸ When problems can't be resolved, they sometimes can be reduced. And you can learn how to help your parent manage them.

▸ Even when things are ultimately "hopeless" you still can influence the quality of your parent's life.

Telling the Truth May Not Always Be Right

CR80

In 1994, it became increasingly difficult for Leila to swallow. Tests to find the problem broke my heart. She had untreatable cancer of the esophagus. The doctor told me that Leila had months to live.

I asked her physicians not to tell Leila the diagnosis yet. My sense was that Leila would not want to know she had cancer. But how could I make sure? I finally devised a strategy that worked. A good friend of ours, Frank, had untreatable lung cancer. One evening, Leila and I talked about Frank. I said I wasn't sure if I would want to know that I had terminal lung cancer. Leila didn't hesitate: "I sure wouldn't want to know if I had cancer!"

Her doctors and I honored her wish. Did she suspect what was wrong? At some level she probably did. However, Leila's memory disorder provided a barrier between her and harsh reality some of the time. This seemed to be one of those times. I hoped that barrier would stay in place all the way to the end. It did.

⚮

The Hospital—
the Battleground:
Making Strategy
a Way of Life

Overview

☙❧

I was giving a presentation to healthcare and social-services professionals. The topic was avoiding unnecessary life changes that result in elders' loss of independence. I call those unnecessary changes "the quantum leap"—for instance, a "leap" from home to nursing home. An audience member raised her hand and said "I see quantum leaps all the time. I am a hospital nurse." I asked her to explain. She said many older people enter her hospital with illnesses or injuries from which they could recover. "They don't because they don't have anyone to help them get back on their feet and return home."

❧☙

This Part is devoted to helping your hospitalized parent avoid the quantum leap.

Opposing Forces within Hospital Walls

You are sending her home?

ᚴᚫᚱᚥ

Leila fainted when she stood up from the commode (portable toilet) next to her bed. I called the rescue squad and went with her to the hospital emergency room. She was given intravenous fluids. After a couple of hours, the ER doctor asked her how she was feeling. She said "Fine." He started to send Leila home. I was alarmed. Why had she fainted? I asked the doctor to have her walk to see what would happen. Leila had gone less than 20 feet when she passed out. The ER staff helped her to the floor. Then the physician admitted her to the hospital.

The next day, Leila was visited by Dr. Brown, her doctor's partner. I told him about the fainting incident in the ER. The second day, her primary physician told us Leila was being discharged. I couldn't believe it. "How can she be discharged? We don't know yet what happened." He answered: "I agree with Dr. Brown. She most likely went to sleep on her commode and fell off." I asked him how he explained the incident in the ER. He looked at me quizzically and asked: "What incident in the ER?"

I told him. He shook his head and kept my mother in the hospital until they figured out why she was fainting. The cause was a side effect of her blood pressure medication.

ᚴᚫᚱᚥ

It was much more than coffee

❦

Another time, Leila was gravely ill with congestive heart failure. She wasn't responding to treatment. I was walking dejectedly down the hospital corridor outside her room when I felt a hand on my arm. It was Becky, one of Leila's nurses. She had been working hard to help Leila survive.

Becky walked with me and said, "Sometimes a patient has to hit 'bottom' before things start to improve. There is still hope." Then she told me there was coffee in the nurses' snack room and that I was welcome to it anytime. If I wanted to keep food in the refrigerator, I could do that, too.

The next morning when I arrived at the hospital, Leila had turned the corner, and was on her way to recovery. When Becky came in later that day, she greeted me with "Guess you won't be drinking our coffee too much longer, huh?"

❦

I always enter a hospital with conflicting emotions. Anxiety is one, and not solely because I am reminded of difficult illnesses and injuries. Leila had hazardous experiences in hospitals that should not have occurred. I also feel comfort, a sense of belonging, because I have met many of the finest people I have known in hospitals: The nurses, aides and other staff that helped Leila live to 89 and also looked out for me.

During the many weeks Leila spent in hospitals at various times, I learned to see them as "battlegrounds." Hospitals were where I helped Leila fight for her life. Our battles were frequently more difficult than they should have been because of mistakes that conspired with her illnesses to threaten Leila's life.

115

Some of the mistakes I learned to watch out for are illustrated in the first story:

▶ Incorrect diagnoses of Leila's medical problems

▶ Poor communications among medical staff

▶ Faulty record-keeping

I believe Leila's labels were partly responsible for at least one mistake. I think her doctor's partner didn't record the ER fainting episode because he thought he knew "what really happened" and my mother didn't because of her advanced age and memory loss.

Our experiences with potentially harmful errors in hospitals were far from unique. In 1999 the Institute for Medicine released a report on the results of two studies on hospital safety. These studies indicate that preventable errors cause at least 44,000 and perhaps as many as 98,000 deaths annually. Deaths due to preventable "adverse events" exceed the deaths attributable to motor vehicle accidents, breast cancer or AIDS. ("To Err is Human: Building a Safer Health System," Institute of Medicine, November 1999.)

In 2006, HealthGrades reported that ". . .recent studies assessing the state of patient safety conclude that current progress is slow. . .and the gap between best possible care and actual care remains large." (Third Annual Patient Safety in American Hospitals Study," April 2006.)

See the Resource Appendix, page 263, for resources to help you improve your parent's safety during hospitalizations.

Fortunately for Leila the mistakes were outweighed by the excellent, and sometimes remarkable, care and support we found in hospitals. Becky, for instance, was one of many nurses who went beyond their job descriptions to help Leila survive. Leila was able to walk until shortly before she died because of a brilliant surgeon who repaired her fractured hip successfully even though her bones were "like Rice Krispies." There are various other examples in this and other chapters of the exceptional care Leila received in hospitals.

I learned to think strategically in almost every situation. Strategy helped me minimize the mistakes. It also helped me to take advantage of the opportunities available to patients and families in hospitals and to ensure that Leila received the best possible care.

The following chapters will prepare you for the strategic battles you will face during your parent's hospitalization.

Chapter 11

Prepare for What Might Happen. Be There When It Does.

Choose the Battleground

To improve the chances of a successful hospitalization, try to prepare for it. If there is more than one hospital near your parents, they may be able to choose between them. If your father's doctor has medical privileges in more than one hospital, which one does the doctor prefer? Which has the best reputation? If your parent has a heart problem, which hospital provides better cardiac care? Nurses are a reliable information source on questions such as these.

Leila preferred the hospital with the most homelike atmosphere. "Friendlier" was the most important factor to her. See the Resource Appendix, page 263, for information on how to determine the quality of services in the hospitals available to your parents.

Don't Keep Important Information to Yourselves

Be sure your parent's doctor and nurses know your parent's choice of hospitals. Their records should include a copy of your parent's advance directive. She should have a copy handy and you should have one. If she has a close neighbor or friend, see if he will keep a copy and get it to the hospital in an emergency. Remember, your parent's records must include a consent form authorizing physicians and hospital staff to discuss her medical care with you.

Keep track of your parent's medications and health conditions so you can share this information with hospital staff. Keep copies of recent laboratory tests and results of other medical procedures. Don't assume hospital staff will have this information in their files. When I eventually got organized, I made sure whoever was at home with Leila knew where these records were.

Join the battle right away

CR&O

I was living in Washington. One of Leila's neighbors called me: Leila was in the hospital with a back injury. She was being treated with muscle relaxants and pain medications. When she had not improved after three disoriented days on these strong medications, Leila had additional X-rays. The original diagnosis was wrong. Leila's hip was fractured.

Leila had surgery on day four. I flew home to be with her. For days after the surgery we didn't know if Leila would recover—not from the fracture, but from the effects of the delay in treatment and the mind-altering medications she didn't need.

CR&O

There are few more important shortcuts back to quality of life than a family's active involvement from the start in a hospitalization, including the emergency room. If you can't be there, is there a capable substitute who can be? This, preferably, would be a person who is empowered to act as your parent's healthcare agent (page 41).

Don't be timid in the emergency room. Let staff know you have power of attorney and important information about your father's health, and that you want to be at his side as soon as possible.

Even staying involved by telephone can make the difference in how the hospital stay turns out. (See "Helping Your Parents Long Distance," page 77.)

Don't Let Sudden Disorientation Panic You

⋘⋙

Leila smiled when I walked into her room. It was her first full day in the hospital. She exclaimed, "I wish you had come sooner! Hope (Leila's sister) was just here." I had just talked on the phone with Hope at her home, 125 miles away, before coming to the hospital.

⋘⋙

It is not unusual for a hospitalized frail older person to lose touch with reality. The first time this happened to Leila, I feared a permanent change. Now I was a seasoned hospital veteran.

Leila's disorientation did not indicate a worsening of her dementia. I had learned from hospital nurses that Leila was in the grip of delirium, or sudden confusion, probably related to her medical condition, strong pain medications and the disorienting hospital environment. A geriatric physician also had informed me that her patients with dementia, such as Leila, were especially prone to acute confusion in hospitals and nursing facilities.

As usual, Leila returned to reality once her pain medication dosage was decreased and her medical condition improved. And, as before, she recovered completely once she was back in her home. Not everyone is as fortunate.

According to the American Geriatrics Society (AGS), "In general, all types of delirium appear strongly associated with poor outcomes among hospitalized patients. These include increased chance of death, complications, long hospital stays, and nursing home care after discharge. Poor outcomes are particularly common among older adults who have long-term delirium. . .

". . .Virtually any medical condition can potentially cause delirium. For example, delirium may be the first sign of a serious, life-threatening illness such as a heart attack. Often, a person has more than one potential medical cause. The most common causes among people in the hospital include problems in bodily fluids, drug reactions, infections, low blood pressure, and low levels of oxygen in the blood. . . It can be the most common complication after surgery in older adults. . ." From the web site of the American Geriatrics Society (AGS) www.healthinaging.org, search for *Delirium*.

▶ *Whenever you notice a change in your parent's mental state tell her nurses and doctors immediately.*

Sudden confusion is a medical emergency. It is essential to treat the underlying causes as soon as possible, as Leila's physicians did. The AGS article provides detailed information on diagnosing and treating this condition.

Ensuring that a vulnerable parent is alone as little as possible during a hospital stay is one key to limiting the impact of sudden confusion. Bring comforting items from home. Leila's colorful, favorite bathrobe was an important part of my confusion-reduction arsenal. If your parent has a hearing or vision problem, tell the staff. Leila's hearing aid was essential to her understanding of what was going on with her care and in the world around her.

Keep "Staph" at Bay

A hospital nurse who reviewed this chapter reminded me that, although it is very important to watch out for the kinds of mistakes discussed earlier in this Part, the most significant hazard in many hospitals is infection. The CDC (Centers for Disease Control and Prevention) reports that in the last 30 years "the proportion of bacteria that is resistant to antibiotics has steeply risen. . .A good example is the type of bacteria that cause "staph" infections–*Staphylococcus aureus*. In 1972, only 2 percent of these types of bacteria were drug resistant.

"By 2004, 63 percent of these types of bacteria had become resistant to the antibiotics commonly used to treat them. . .Staph infections. . .are a growing problem in hospitals and healthcare facilities such as nursing homes . . ." (CDC press release, October 19, 2006, "CDC Urges Hospitals and Health-care Facilities to Increase Efforts to Reduce Drug-Resistant Infections.")

Another CDC press release reports "The main mode of transmission (of staph bacteria) to other patients is through. . .hands, especially healthcare workers' hands. Hands may become contaminated with. . . bacteria by contact with infected or colonized patients (those who carry staph bacteria but are not infected).

"If appropriate hand hygiene such as washing with soap and water or using an alcohol-based hand sanitizer is not performed, the bacteria can be spread when the healthcare worker touches other patients." ("MRSA in Healthcare Settings," October 6, 2006) "MRSA" stands for "Methicillin-resistant staphylococcus aureous."

You can find these press releases on the CDC web page: www.cdc.gov. Search for *"2006 Infections in Hospitals"*. You will find an October 19, 2006 release on infections in hospitals.

I was concerned constantly about staph infections when Leila was hospitalized. Drug resistant does not necessarily mean "untreatable," but, given Leila's frailty, I was afraid she would not survive the staph battle. Consequently, I frequently was bouncing between "Leila needs one more day to be ready to go home" and "But it is one more day of vulnerability to staph infection."

The hospital nurse who stressed the importance of infection control told me that the rules for visitors in her hospital include:

▶ Do not visit the patient when you are ill.

▶ Wear a protective mask (provided by hospital staff) when you are sick, if a visit is imperative.

▶ Wash your hands when you arrive and when you leave.

Many hospitals are developing aggressive infection control programs. You will not insult a physician or nurse if you ask about the hospital's program, and, specifically, what the rules are for hand washing. Emphasize your concern about protecting your parent's safety.

For more advice on avoiding infections in hospitals visit the Yale University Hospital Elder Life Program web site. The easiest way to get there is an Internet search for: _The Hospital Elder Life Program_.

Chapter 12

Establish Your Authority

Let staff know you wish to participate in decisions regarding your parent's treatment. Be clear about how involved you wish to be. I wanted to be consulted whenever a doctor recommended a medication change, a diagnostic procedure, or change in the treatment plan. If something happened in the middle of the night I wanted to be called immediately.

I was not Leila's guardian. She was legally entitled to make her own treatment decisions. However, her memory disorder made it difficult for her to do that even in normal circumstances. In the hospital it was impossible. Nevertheless, if I hadn't asked hospital staff to contact me about any aspect of Leila's treatment and health status, some important decisions would have been made without me. If you live at a distance, ask nurses and physicians to involve you in these decisions by telephone.

Remember, even if you are your parent's healthcare agent, if she is capable of making sound decisions about her care, you will need her permission before hospital staff will discuss her case with you.

Be the Family Member People Want to Help

C3 80

I was talking to a nursing home aide about the role of family members in improving the quality of life of parents in that facility. She agreed that we can make a major difference, but "unfortunately, the involved families are usually the ones that yell at us all the time. We run when we see them coming."

CR 80

In the hospital, the nursing home or your own home, being unpleasant to those who provide important services to your parent is not smart. You want them to listen to you and work with you, not avoid you. Ideally, at least some will become allies. Chapter 5, "Take Advantage of Your Natural Resources" and Chapter 9, "Making Things Happen" emphasize strategies for working well with providers of services. Because hospitalizations often begin with a crisis, a reminder here of a strategic approach to follow even in the worst and most disorienting circumstances:

▶ Be friendly and respectful to everyone even if they don't return the favor.

▶ Tone it down. I tried hard, even in the most urgent circumstances, to stay as calm as I could. Or at least to appear calm even though I was churning on the inside.

▶ But don't back down. Taking a stand on behalf of your parent, when you know what you are doing, will increase staff respect for you and your cause. If hospital staff like you, or at least don't dislike you, and if their anxieties don't rise when they see you coming, they are more likely to cooperate with you even when you are being an assertive family member.

Help Shape the Battle Plan

Your dad has just been admitted to a hospital room. Nurses and aides are moving briskly through the halls. Doctors are talking with them, looking at patients' charts, moving in and out of the patients' rooms. Your father is disoriented and so are you. What do you do? Where do you start?

Be sure the admission records are correct

In addition to providing the name of your father's physician, your father's age, occupation, marital status, and place of residence, these records also should include information such as:

- ▶ Advance directive

- ▶ Medical conditions other than the one(s) causing hospitalization

- ▶ Recent hospitalizations

- ▶ Previous surgical procedures (operations)

- ▶ Medications your parent was taking before admission and the dosages

- ▶ Medication allergies

- ▶ Blood type

- ▶ Emergency contacts

- ▶ Names of the people authorized by your parent to act as his healthcare agents

If the admitting nurse does not ask these questions, volunteer this information. Tell nursing staff other facts they should know. Leila had "dementia" listed as one of her medical conditions. I had the record clarified: "Not Alzheimer's. But unable to remember important details or understand complicated questions."

Brief the newcomers

In some hospitals the family doctor is not in charge of her patients' care. These hospitals employ physicians who work only in the hospital. This may or may not work to your parent's advantage. One thing is certain: This physician will need assistance to learn what she needs to know about him.

Put this guide's medical problem-solving steps into action

Be there when your parent's doctor is in the hospital to see patients. This is important not only at first, but as much as possible throughout the stay. Hospital staff will have only a general idea of when the doctor will see him. Sometimes they will be able to tell you if the physician is in the hospital. For more precise information, call the physician's office and ask about her schedule.

The doctor is likely to be moving fast. Don't be daunted. Volunteer information. Ask questions, even if you need to follow her into the hospital corridor to do it. I usually asked:

- ▶ What is the doctor's diagnosis at this point?

- ▶ What tests will be ordered, if any?

- ▶ What treatment has she ordered?

- ▶ What medications is Leila supposed to be taking? Why?

- ▶ What is the customary hospital stay for elders with this medical problem? I wanted a general idea so l would not be surprised with "We are sending your mother home tomorrow."

If you cannot be there and there is no "substitute you," work with the physician and the hospital nurses by telephone.

▶ *If the doctor has not ordered medications your parent has been taking at home make sure this is not a mistake.*

Meet the discharge planner ASAP

Early in your parent's hospital stay you may not have time to think much about what happens next. Hospitals have social workers called discharge planners whose job is to help patients prepare to leave. Their jobs can be hectic. It's best to get them thinking about your situation before the plan becomes an urgent matter.

Seek Out the Hospital's Lifesaving Forces

Why not the best?

CԐ৪১

During one of Leila's most difficult battles with congestive heart failure, her primary physician told me she was not responding to treatment. He was going to ask a cardiologist to visit her that afternoon. I asked him which physician would be seeing her. "Dr. Green." By then I had done some networking. Dr. Green's partner had an outstanding reputation. I asked, "May we have Dr. Smith instead?"

Leila's doctor hesitated, then said that was fine but Dr. Smith would not be seeing patients until the next day. I asked whether that would put Leila at risk. He didn't think so. Dr. Smith began treating Leila the next morning. Getting him involved was a key to saving her life.

CԐ৪১

Your parent is hospitalized and is not improving. If his primary physician does not bring in a specialist, ask her to do so. Leila's physicians were always supportive of my (reasonable) suggestions, such as "Can we do more to help my mother strengthen her lungs?" In this case her doctor ordered respiratory therapy from staff trained to help patients recover lung capacity.

Mine the hospital gold

I found a wealth of information during Leila's hospital stays by observing specialists and asking them questions. I told friends that some days it seemed as if I was going to school in the hospital. For instance, the physicians and therapists who specialized in rehabilitation medicine did not accept "old" as a reason for giving up. They saw my mother's strengths and potential, not just her injuries and illnesses. With each new instructive experience, I became a better advocate for Leila.

No hospital staff members were more important to Leila's survival and my state of mind than the nurses who cared for her. Once I realized how difficult a hospital stay can be, I kept a journal. One entry summed up what the nurses meant to us: *"Hospital nurses. . .our great information resource. . .my mom's advocates. . .my therapists."*

Hospitals provide services and educational seminars to help people manage Medicare bills and stay healthy when they are *not* hospitalized. They advertise community education activities in the newspaper.

Managing urgent problems and root causes in hospitals

An example:

Your father is in the hospital with a broken hip. You are looking for a nursing home where he can receive effective physical therapy after he is discharged. While it might be helpful to have this information later on, first go back to the beginning:

▶ Work on the urgent problem. Do everything possible to help your father regain as much strength and mobility as he can while he is hospitalized. If he hasn't yet had surgery, the urgent problem may be finding the best surgeon. What you are able to help him accomplish in the hospital will have much to do with what that next step needs to be.

▶ Look for root causes. Why did your father fall? Does he have problems with dizziness or his balance? Those are problems that can be worked on in the hospital and after he is discharged. Did his hip break because of fragile bones? Maybe treatment for this condition could begin now.

Chapter 13

Never Let Your Guard Down

Be on guard to protect your parent from the harm caused by mistakes that occur in hospitals. The kinds of errors described in this chapter were made by medical staff who wanted to provide good care to Leila. None were intentional. You may not encounter any of these kinds of mistakes. It is best, however, to be prepared.

Take Nothing for Granted

Is twice better than once?

ಚಿఖీ

The morning after Leila was admitted with her heart condition, I got to the hospital early. She was being wheeled out of her room. I asked where they were taking her. A nurse told me, "She is going for back X-rays." I asked her if she knew Leila had back X-rays in the ER. "She did?" The nurse called the ER. Then she returned Leila to her room.

I had helped Leila avoid an unnecessary and very unpleasant experience. X-ray procedures that required her to lie still on hard surfaces were painful for her because of her bone disease.

CRED

It was *not* about communications?

CRED

Later that day I mentioned to a staff member at the nursing station for my mother's floor how bad communications had been. She replied, "Oh, it's not a communications problem. It's just that one doctor will often not know what the other doctor has done."

CRED

Some lessons learned from such experiences:

▸ Sometimes doctors don't involve the family of memory-impaired patients or their nurses in discussions with these patients. Make certain they have complete information on your parent's medical history, including what has happened in the hospital, to ensure accurate assessments—and avoid unnecessary procedures.

▸ If a doctor orders a particular plan of treatment, find out directly from the physician what it is. Then check on what hospital staff and other doctors think the treatment plan is. I learned "not everything gets into the record."

From my journal:

Stay on top of communications!

Look out for putting into action what has been ordered. Doc changes meds, in conversation, but mistakenly orders the old med anyway.

It's good to double-check everything in the hospital...the meds... the schedules...when the X-ray is coming...what the X-ray is for.

Don't trust that every doctor will read your parents' medical records on what has happened before or after they were hospitalized.

Some hospital staff don't have thorough knowledge of what they are doing with the patient. They either don't read the files or the files are not complete.

In case you still need convincing

CB80

Leila needed a chest X–ray. I told her nurse that she'd had one at the other hospital a few months before. I wondered if it would be helpful to have that test result. She said it would be. She asked me to get it for them. "If we have it sent here, it will probably be lost." I asked if I should leave it at the main desk for that hospital floor. "Oh, no, don't do that! We will never see it again. Please hand it directly to one of us (nurses)."

CB80

Always Watch the Medications

CB80

I learned that a physician new to Leila's case had prescribed a drug that had made her ill during a prior hospital visit. This information was highlighted in her hospital medical records. His mistake was inexcusable. Leila could not have been expected to recall this experience. Her nurse apologized, called the physician, and he ordered a medication Leila could tolerate.

CB80

In July of 2006, the Institute of Medicine (IOM) reported that "In hospitals, medication errors occur during every step of the medication process: prescribing it, dispensing it, administering it, and monitoring its impact—but they occur most frequently during the prescribing and administering stages... However, substantial variations in error rates are found across facilities..." ("Preventing Medication Errors: Quality Chasm Series," IOM, July 20, 2006.)

Some things to keep in mind:

▶ Stay on top of medications every day, especially when a new physician enters the picture. This includes learning the purpose of any new prescription.

▶ If a parent has responded poorly to a certain drug, be sure it is noted in her records. Then be sure all her nurses know it including those on the overnight shift.

▶ Double-check the side effects of any medication prescribed for your parent and whether it reacts negatively with other drugs she may be taking.

▶ Watch to see if medications are given as scheduled. Time demands on nurses sometimes make it difficult for them to keep to that schedule.

The IOM report recommends that "Patients should understand more about their medications and take more responsibility for monitoring those medications...Doctors, nurses, pharmacists and other providers...should inform their patients fully about the risks, contraindications, and possible side effects of the medications they are taking and what to do if they experience a side effect."

Go to the IOM web site for more information on preventing medication errors: www.iom.edu. Click on *Reports*, then on the *"Preventing Medication Errors"* report. Scroll down to *"Fact Sheet: What You Can Do to Prevent Medication Errors."*

Physicians and hospitals are working to correct these errors. Nevertheless, it is best to act as though no medications management system exists.

Chapter 14

Work on the Labels Right Away

"Do Not Resuscitate" (DNR)

 C3&O

    Leila was admitted to the hospital one evening because of a back injury. I returned early the next morning. The head nurse intercepted me on my way to Leila's room. She wanted me to know that Leila was "in congestive heart failure." Then the nurse told me that she had obtained a "verbal directive" from Leila that she did not want to be revived if her heart should stop.

    I could not believe what I had just heard. If my mother's heart was failing, it was probably because of recent medication changes, not because she was terminally ill. Although she was 84, slowed by memory loss and beaten up by osteoporosis, Leila still loved life. She would not turn away from it so readily.

    I went to Leila's room with the nurse. There lay my mother—in body only. The nurse had obtained a DNR "consent" from a patient who was orbiting Saturn on a Demerol injection (strong painkiller). I pointed this out to the nurse and told her to reverse her DNR directive. I asked her to have the doctor

137

prescribe a less-potent pain medication. This one had paralyzed Leila's body and her capacity to look out for herself.

Unfortunately, I did not know what I know now. I did not yet have healthcare power of attorney authorizing me to act on Leila's behalf in this kind of situation. I went to the cafeteria for a cup of coffee and returned to find that Leila had been given another Demerol injection. She was back in full orbit. The head nurse had not agreed with my assessment of what was in Leila's best interest and had disregarded my wishes.

CRSO

This was one of those times when getting "really angry," as one of the nurses described it later, was the best strategy. (Not that I thought about it in advance.) Leila was switched to a pain medication that did not disorient her and gradually came back to life.

A conversation with other nurses on my mother's floor helped me to understand what Leila and I were dealing with. I learned that several of them would not want to be revived if they were old and sick in the hospital. They had seen too many patients brought back from the brink of death only to linger in a "vegetative state." Because of Leila's back injury, she had not been to her hair salon in the days before her hospitalization. As she lay in her hospital bed, without makeup, pale, ill and disoriented, I could see how Leila might be mistaken for a patient who had "had it" and was ready to die. *"Old, sick, confused, crippled . . . Who would want to go on like this?"*

Here's what I learned about what to do in similar circumstances:

Protect Your Parent's "First Class Citizenship"

I reminded the nurses that whether or not Leila should be revived was her choice, no one else's. She had not been able to understand her choices because of her disorientation. I told them that Leila valued her life and that I expected her to be given the same chances younger patients would be given to make it out of there alive and mobile. I asked them to tell that to the nurses on the next shift. It was a civil conversation, with a touch of tension in the air.

Get Your Parent into the Battle

As I said earlier, Leila was my "secret weapon" in these kinds of situations. I had to get her going on stripping away the labels and false assumptions that may have blinded some staff to who she was. Once her pain medication was changed, her beautiful smile returned. Soon she was asking questions about nurses' lives, and talking about hers. *"So you don't live in a nursing home, Mrs. Lynch?"* A friend fixed her hair. Leila got her makeup on and sat up in a colorful robe. I brought in a scrapbook of pictures covering her tomboy childhood, her active life as a homemaker and teacher, and her fulfilling retirement.

Be Helpful to Hospital Staff

An effective strategy for getting hospital staff as involved as possible in the care of your parent is to do things that make their work less demanding. And their work is often very demanding. When it was time to help Leila get out of bed and into a chair, I often did that, when it was not risky to attempt it. I helped her with meals and sometimes with her baths. Several nurses told me they appreciated my assistance.

My (usually) friendly relationship with nurses made it easy for me to stay with Leila before and after regular visiting hours. No doctor or nurse questioned why I was still there at 11 p.m. When the main entrance was closed, I went in through the emergency room entry.

Promote a Campaign Atmosphere

I asked friends and neighbors to start visiting Leila as soon as she was ready to see them. At least one or two came each day. I paid self-employed nurses' aides to help her with her meals when I couldn't be there. Her room filled with cards and flowers. With their actions and words, Leila's friends let hospital staff know *"This is a person of value. Something very important is going on here."*

I told nurses, aides, doctors, physical therapists and social work staff how appreciative I was of their services to my mother and how important they were to her quality of life. I noticed nurses and aides begin to make extra visits to Leila's room "to be sure she finished her pudding" or to get her to walk around her room one more time.

One morning, the nurse who had put "Do not resuscitate" on Leila's chart walked past her room. She called out "Who is doing Leila's hair today?" My mother had surfaced, the labels had been torn away and the campaign was rolling.

"You knew her."

CB&O

Fifteen days after Leila entered the hospital, she came home. Sara, one of the hospital nurses, checked Leila out and helped get her to the car. Sara had been one of the many nurses whose care had been so important to my mother's survival, but she was a quiet person. I wasn't sure how she felt about me, given my early conflicts with other nurses.

As Sara walked away, I thanked her for all she and the other nurses had done to help Leila get well and leave the hospital. Sara whirled around to tell me what had been bottled up: "We didn't get your mother out of here. You did. You fought for her." She apologized for the lack of cooperation I encountered when I tried to change Leila's pain medication to something less potent.

Then Sara said: "You knew her. We didn't."

CB&O

Chapter 15

Beware the Self-fulfilling "Hopeless" Assessment

ॐ

After several days of Leila's treatment for congestive heart failure, and before the campaign gained momentum, Dr. ___, a lung specialist, told me: "Your mother is gravely ill. She has not been taking in enough nutrition to allow her to recover. She probably wouldn't do well with a feeding tube inserted through her nose into her stomach. We want to keep her comfortable."

I was stunned. I hadn't realized that Leila had not been eating enough. The physician was telling me I should accept that she probably was going to die as a consequence. I told the doctor (somewhat sarcastically): "I have an idea. Why don't we get her to eat?" He asked me what I had in mind. I asked him, "Isn't there a food specialist we could call?" And I told him that if he had informed my mother she had to eat more to save her life she would have eaten more.

Within fifteen minutes the hospital dietitian was in Leila's room. She was optimistic. "I will whip up a high-octane pudding. It will be tasty and

141

loaded with calories and protein. A little goes a long way. We will send up a fresh batch with each meal." Then she told me, "I am happy you contacted me. We don't always get called in time."

I devoted the next couple of days to getting Leila to eat that pudding which she did find tasty. I kept telling her "If you want to get out of here, how about one more spoonful?" As she got better, she would beat me to the punch: "I know. One more mouthful and I will get out of here."

I called the dietitian to tell her she had saved my mother's life. Leila lived four more happy years, still eating her lifesaving pudding, and did not return to the hospital until a few months before she died.

CR&O

Journal entries:

> *If Leila declines to eat a meal, no one gets alarmed. Little time to work with her on it.*

> *If there are problems with nutrition, or potential problems, have meals with the person . . . bring in friends . . . doesn't mean you have to eat what the patients eat (grin).*

> *Get to know the dietitian!! People can die just from not having people focused on getting them to eat, not because "it's time."*

Chapter 16

Exit Strategy

Medicare and Medicaid usually do not reimburse hospitals for the full cost of a patient's care. Consequently, hospitals try to keep patient stays as brief as possible. The pressure to discharge older patients is not related, usually, to "making money," but to limiting financial loss. Nevertheless, you should assume that this pressure will be running under the surface of each hospital visit.

I wanted Leila out of the hospital, too, but not before she was well enough to leave. Several times, hospital staff were pushing for discharge and I was pushing to keep her there a little longer. I was successful when I could make arguments that convinced physicians it would be harmful to send her home. Once I asked Leila's physical therapist to make clear in his notes that Leila wasn't ready for discharge. He did and it worked. When I was not successful, I had to move fast to set up homecare.

Medicare requires the hospital to offer your parent the right to appeal a discharge decision if you believe he is too ill or impaired to leave. The hospital must provide a pamphlet detailing the appeal process. Your father must appeal before noon on the day after he receives a required Notice of Non-Coverage.

Ask hospital social workers to help with the appeal. If there is a Patient Representative on staff, she will assist you throughout the appeal process. Regardless of the outcome, Medicare will pay the hospital charges during the process, which usually takes at least 24 hours.

Focus on the Flame

Your parent may be able to return home directly from the hospital. However, his medical condition may make it impossible for him to get along at home for a while or you may not be able to find the necessary support services. Whatever the next step, use what you are learning in this guide to keep your parent's flame of motivation burning.

Review What You Have Going for You. Do What You Can

If it is *at all* possible, try to work out a plan for taking your parent home—his or yours. I know several elders who "would not comply" with a nursing home's physical therapy plan yet got back on their feet soon after returning home. Your parent's discharge planner may not have much time to help you and your parent prepare to leave. This guide can help you work with the planner to develop a feasible and creative plan. *If you do not have time to read this guide, have a family member or friend do it for you.* Almost everything in this book applies to planning for discharge. Of course, each chapter in "Helping Your Parent Remain At Home" is vital to sound planning. Remember, families are often the deciding factor in whether or not elders get well and strong enough to return home.

If a nursing home is the only reasonable option, network in advance to find a place noted for its care and services. The discharge planner should help you find the one that best suits your parent. The hospital may have a "sub-acute" unit to which he may be transferred instead of a nursing home if you wish. Nurses often will be your most valuable information source about the quality of the places you are considering.

Before your parent leaves the hospital, review this checklist with the discharge nurse and discharge planner. A friend with a chronic illness that has put her in many hospitals over 20 years worked with me on this list. It combines our knowledge of what it takes to avoid omissions or mistakes that can make going home more difficult than it needs to be:

▶ What is the plan of treatment after leaving the hospital?

▶ If a homecare agency will be involved: Who is the contact person? What is the plan for the agency's involvement?

▶ Is the medical equipment you will need at home ready, such as a hospital bed and portable toilet?

▶ What are the activity restrictions at home?

▶ What medications have been prescribed? What are they for? What are the potential side effects? Has the pharmacy been contacted? Make sure you have the medications list when you leave.

▶ What other kinds of supplies or personal items might be helpful at home? Which ones can be prescribed by the doctor and are covered by Medicare or Medicaid?

▶ Are there diet or fluid restrictions?

▶ What is the best diet to follow at home?

▶ What kinds of warning symptoms should you watch for that indicate complications related to your parent's medical condition? What do you do when you notice them? Go to the emergency room? Call your doctor?

You have heard this before: Take nothing important for granted.

Helping Your Parents Remain at Home—Even in Challenging Circumstances

Overview

Much of this guide builds a foundation for helping your parents remain as healthy, content and self-reliant as possible wherever they live. This Part focuses on what else you should know in order to help them remain in their own homes even when times get tough.

Is a *place* the answer?

ॐ

It was another crisis. Back to the emergency room again. The ER physician looked Leila over, checked her records, then asked me to talk with him privately. He would run some tests on her heart function, but then we should discuss ". . .the ultimate resolution of this case."

That evening, I sat next to Leila as she slept in her hospital bed and reflected on that chilling discussion in the ER. After years of helping her survive medical crises, I was a seasoned veteran when it came to misguided advice from those who should know better. It always shocked me, nevertheless. The "ultimate resolution" to Leila Lynch's medical problem was not medical care, but a place. Not a specific place. Just anywhere called "nursing home."

I had stifled my reflex response to the doctor's suggestion and told him my mother was doing just fine where she was, in the home where she had lived for 50 years. I asked him to focus on Leila's medical problems. He shrugged, said "OK," ran some tests, and had her admitted.

CRISO

In Chapter 2 you will find stories about my Aunt Alvira and the grandmother of an acquaintance of mine named Rob. Aunt Alvira's home, and her stairs, kept her going when everyone else believed she "belonged" in a nursing home. Returning to a place she could call home was the spark Rob's grandmother needed to choose surgery and get back on her feet. For Leila and these two women, being home was not only the result of maintaining control over life, it was the key to succeeding at it.

It is no secret that most of us feel the same way about home. Home is where we want to be in old age. It is where we can remain most comfortable and in control. In this Part, I share more of what I learned about helping our parents get what they want in their later years.

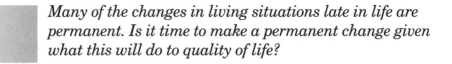

Many of the changes in living situations late in life are permanent. Is it time to make a permanent change given what this will do to quality of life?

Chapter 17

Think Big. . .and Take Small Steps

Set Your Goals High and Make Bold, Hopeful Plans

Thinking Big is the driving force behind hope. It means help your parents hold on to what they cherish, even when others may think it is not possible. Keep that flame burning as brightly as you can.

When Leila was hospitalized with a broken pelvis early in our years together, we set the goal that was the most inspiring and uplifting to each of us. Against the advice of the hospital discharge planner we decided to try physical therapy for Leila in our home. What was the worst likely outcome? She would go to a nursing home later than she otherwise would have.

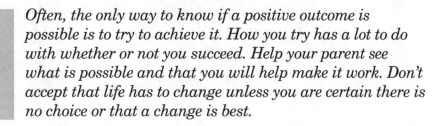 *Often, the only way to know if a positive outcome is possible is to try to achieve it. How you try has a lot to do with whether or not you succeed. Help your parent see what is possible and that you will help make it work. Don't accept that life has to change unless you are certain there is no choice or that a change is best.*

Setting goals must be realistic. Planning for something that is unattainable can be heartbreaking and dangerous. Leila's memory disorder made it impossible for her to manage daily life without assistance. Dr. Swenson, a skilled geriatric physician, told me there was a good chance Leila would get back on her feet with lots of help.

We knew the plan might not work. But it was worth trying. For the next nine years I helped Leila set hopeful, sometimes unconventional, goals. We understood that setting our sights too low would mean we might never know how much we still could accomplish.

Think Big means you should not avoid major surgery or other difficult medical treatments just because of age. Rob's grandmother overcame her own misconceptions about what was possible at her age and agreed to surgical repair of her hip even though she was 82.

The author on the porch of the family home with his mother (right) and her sister, Hope—in another era.

Remaining at home or in "homelike" places can be the motivation a parent needs to remain as strong and vital as possible. Home has the power to heal.

Take Small Steps

Take Small Steps is the close companion of Think Big. It means

▶ assist your parents to limit the changes in their lives to what is absolutely necessary.

▶ do not make unwanted life-altering decisions until you are sure there are not less drastic and less costly choices.

Overnight help

☙❧

Mary's mother, Jean, had been hospitalized with an injury and recently had been discharged. She was doing well on her own during the day but had fallen one night on her way to the bathroom. Jean was not afraid to be alone and preferred maintaining her privacy at night. Mary was concerned that Jean might be injured and no one would know. Mary wondered where she could get overnight help. Because her mother was not afraid of being alone, I suggested she should:

- *Set Jean up with a hospital lifeline emergency response system.*

- *Keep a commode (portable toilet) at Jean's bedside at night.*

☙❧

Take small steps means more than "don't move unless you have to." Don't do more or spend more than you must to make a living situation comfortable and safe. Jean's goal was to continue to live as normally as possible. Leaving her alone with a commode next to her bed was riskier than having overnight help. But it reduced risk substantially, saved money and avoided an unwelcome intrusion into Jean's life. Jean did not have a problem with confusion. If she did, then a "bigger step" (overnight aide) might have been the way to go.

Small-step-low-cost community services

Many programs and services that can help your parents remain at home can also save them money. Some services are cost-free. They vary across communities and can be scarce in rural areas. Learning what is available is not difficult. The first contacts should be with your parents' Key Resources, page 248.

The services available to your parents may include:

▶ Transportation

▶ Housing, including help with financing, maintenance and renters' assistance

▶ Home weatherization

▶ Energy Assistance, including help with utility and heating bills

▶ Chore services, such as assistance with repairs, lawn and sidewalk maintenance, light housekeeping

▶ Telephone and friendly visitor contact

▶ Meal services and nutrition education

▶ Food stamps

▶ Senior centers (described in "Making the Most of This Guide," page xiv)

▶ Public health services

▶ Telephone companies' special needs programs

- ▶ Financial counseling, including pension counseling

- ▶ Legal assistance

- ▶ Self-help support groups

- ▶ Employment assistance

- ▶ Crime Prevention/Victim Assistance

- ▶ Volunteering opportunities

- ▶ Physical fitness programs

- ▶ Elder abuse and neglect intervention, including self-neglect

- ▶ Family counseling

You will find more complete descriptions of these and other community services at the web site of the federal Administration on Aging: www.aoa.gov. Click on *Services for Seniors*.

Remember that neighbors and other friends can often be the most helpful "community service providers."

Cost-saving national and state programs

- ▶ www.usa.gov is a federal government web site that you *must* visit. The introduction to its web page sums up what it offers: "Whatever you want or need from the U.S. government, it's here . . .You'll find a rich treasure of online information, services and resources." Click on *Senior Citizens' Resources*.

- ▶ Benefits Checkup is a joint service of the National Council on Aging and the federal government. It assists people age 55 and older to connect to government and private programs that can help them pay for healthcare, utility costs and other needs. On average there are 50 to 70 such programs in each state. www.benefitscheckup.org

Both of these resources include information on services available to residents of rural areas.

▶ Benefits Checkup Rx helps older adults receiving Medicare reduce the costs of prescription drugs. It will assist them to figure out if they qualify for Extra Help under Medicare prescription drug coverage and will also direct them to other potential sources of assistance with medication costs. www.benefitscheckuprx.org

▶ Partnership for Patient Assistance is an alliance of pharmaceutical companies, healthcare providers and patient advocacy organizations that assists consumers to find inexpensive medications and free healthcare clinics. www.pparx.org

▶ NeedyMeds is a non-profit organization focused on helping people who cannot afford medicine or other healthcare costs. This information includes help for some people with specific diseases and other medical conditions. www.needymeds.com

When these kinds of services no longer are enough, the next step might be homecare, which is discussed in the following chapter.

Chapter 18

Finding In-Home Helpers in *All* the Right Places

Leila received substantial government financial assistance in order to remain at home. You may not need or be able to afford the amount of in-home help Leila and I had. I describe our experience in detail to familiarize you with your options. The kinds of assistance I found are available in most communities. However, residents of rural areas often will have to rely substantially on the "informal" community networks I describe here and in Chapter 5.

What is Homecare?

Homecare refers to services that help people remain at home when they otherwise might not be able to. These services continue to expand as our population ages. They include

▶ Health services

Home healthcare includes a remarkable range of services that includes nursing care under a physician's orders, help from a home-health aide, physical and speech therapy, intravenous medical treatment, and assistance with managing medications.

This is a very short list of available health services.

▶ Assistance with personal care activities

Personal care aides assist people with Activities of Daily Living (commonly known as "ADLs"). ADLs include bathing, dressing, grooming, transferring to or from beds and chairs, walking, eating, and using the toilet.

▶ Homemaker and chore services

These services include meal preparation, laundry, light housekeeping and shopping (and more.)

▶ Companion and volunteer services

Some agencies offer their clients companionship for which they pay by the hour. Some also offer the no-cost companionship of volunteers.

▶ Assistance with managing everyday life

These services range from making appointments and running errands to caring for pets and houseplants.

▶ Social work assistance

The help provided by social workers, sometimes known as "care managers," includes finding community services, setting up in-home care plans and dealing with government benefits and insurance issues.

▶ Transportation

These services include help with shopping and getting to medical and other appointments. Liability issues prevent some homecare agencies from providing transportation. However, they can help their clients find transportation assistance.

Providers of Homecare Services

These providers include

▶ A variety of homecare organizations. Check with each to learn which kinds of services it offers. Only certain agencies are licensed by state government to provide in-home health services. The agencies that provide these services are usually also licensed to provide healthcare covered by Medicare and Medicaid.

▶ Private-duty nurses. Find out whether they are licensed to offer services funded by Medicare or Medicaid.

▶ Medical equipment retailers. Some are licensed to sell or rent equipment covered by Medicare and Medicaid. Some pharmacies sell equipment and other products that assist with in-home care.

▶ Self-employed caregivers.

How We Paid for Our In-Home Help

Low and middle-income families will find that some homecare services, such as healthcare by nurses and home-health aides, are not affordable for long.

Medicare occasionally provided Leila some nursing and aide assistance, but only when she required skilled care—for instance to help her through an acute illness.

The state Medicaid program that gave us long-term help is known as the Home and Community Based Services (HCBS) program. (I also discuss Medicaid in Chapter 4.) This program enabled us to receive help from a homecare agency and also to hire some of our caregivers directly. Without the support of the HCBS program, I would have had to spend much of my life savings to help Leila remain at home.

Unfortunately, there are long waiting lists in most states for help from HCBS programs because of limited funds. It is bewildering that Medicaid funds are readily available for nursing home care but usually not for sufficient in-home assistance, especially since homecare is often less costly. Even with ample government support, Leila and I saved the taxpayer around $10,000 a year by making homecare work for us.

States are slowly developing programs designed to provide in-home services to all Medicaid recipients at risk of having to move to a nursing home. The emphasis is on "slowly." The people who receive this assistance are commonly referred to as "consumers."

Most of these programs are working toward

▶ Increased funding for in-home services.

▶ Consumer control over the kinds of help they receive, who provides it, and when. This control extends to hiring, scheduling and managing their caregivers to the extent that they want and can handle this responsibility.

▶ Reduction of Medicaid costs.

Consumer control of services is known by various terms, such as self-directed services, consumer- directed services, and person-centered services. Leila and I, essentially, had a self-directed service plan, which is described later in this chapter.

In Wisconsin the Partnership program pays for and coordinates healthcare and long-term care services for its participants. Family Care combines funds from a variety of programs into one flexible long-term care consumer benefit. Both programs are developing the self-directed services option. Neither program operates statewide.

Colorado's In-Home Support Services program (IHSS) enables Medicaid consumers to direct, select and train their own caregivers. IHSS also covers healthcare and assists consumers to improve their independent living skills.

Innovative Programs of All-inclusive Care for the Elderly (PACE) provide health and long-term care services to Medicaid consumers, but there are fewer than 50 PACE sites in the United States.

Check with your parents' Key Resources, page 248, to learn whether these kinds of programs are available to them. The program names will vary across states.

Much of the rest of this chapter discusses what I learned that can help you get along without assistance from government programs and without nightmarish expenses.

Leila, Terry and Homecare: The Beginning

Sometimes privacy needs to be redefined

CR80

Leila was resting on her hospital bed in the dining room. It was noon. I had helped her with her bath and prepared her breakfast. Now I was upstairs, involved in an urgent work project. Leila called out to me, wondering if I would help her walk to the front porch. I asked her to hang on for just a while more.

Then it hit me. Neither of us had wanted strangers in our home to help with her care. But we both were suffering in this situation. I was racing between caregiving and my work. She was lying on her bed far too much. Leila was getting weaker and I was a very tired guy.

I went down to the dining room and suggested we find someone to help us out. She agreed. It was a life-transforming decision.

CR80

Within a few months we had several "strangers" in our home. Within a year we had many. First I'll tell you who they were. Then I'll tell you how I found them and how you can do the same.

Who Helped Us at Home

Homecare agency staff

The people who first assisted us worked for a local agency. In the first year, before she qualified for Medicaid, Leila spent most of her savings on that agency's services. I spent some of my own. It was worth it. Their staff made it possible for us to figure out a new way of life. They included

- ▶ Registered Nurses (RNs) who monitored Leila's medical conditions, supervised agency home-health aides and therapists, and taught me some basic nursing skills, such as how to prevent bed sores.

- ▶ Home-health aides, also known as certified nursing assistants or CNAs, who helped Leila maintain her health and mobility, assisted her with bathing, grooming and other personal care needs (activities of daily living) and also helped with laundry, prepared some meals, and provided companionship.

- ▶ Personal care workers who also helped with activities of daily living and housekeeping. Personal care workers are not certified to assist RNs with healthcare.

- ▶ Physical therapists who came to our home when Leila needed skilled help to strengthen her arms and legs or improve her balance. Her physician ordered this additional care. Most of the costs for this therapy were covered by Medicare. If you believe your parents might benefit from physical therapy, see if their doctor will order it.

The agency's CNAs or personal care workers were in our home daily for several hours during the work week throughout the rest of Leila's life. The RNs visited a few times a month, unless Leila was ill or required physical therapy. RN hourly rates are much higher than hourly aide rates. However, if your parent does not need skilled care, such as physical therapy, wound care or intravenous medical treatments, RN visits will be relatively infrequent.

Respite volunteers

Respite services give family caregivers a break from their daily routines. Many communities have organizations whose volunteers provide respite in families' homes. Some organizations charge fees. Nursing homes and other residential facilities sometimes provide respite care.

The respite organization in Racine sent volunteers to us for several hours a week, at no cost. This assistance was primarily companionship, although the volunteers assisted Leila to walk and use the toilet safely.

One volunteer, Marie, came to our home for seven years. On each visit, I went out to dinner by myself or spent time with friends. Those moments were precious and revitalizing. Marie and Leila became good friends. I will always be grateful for what she did for us.

Independent in-home caregivers

Some days, Leila and I needed many hours of help at home. Some days only a few. It depended on my schedule and workload. Eventually, as our lives stabilized, Leila and I began hiring aides who worked for themselves and who could work varied hours.

These independent caregivers eventually gave Leila most of the help she needed. However, although their hourly rates were lower than the homecare agency's, we did not discontinue our agency's services. We did not want to lose the support and peace of mind provided us by its excellent nurses and caregivers.

Our independent caregivers were

▶ Self-employed aides who were trained to provide homecare, or

▶ Caregivers trained by me.
Much of what Leila needed was not healthcare but personal care from reliable, compassionate people with common sense. I found women fitting that description who wanted part-time work and flexible schedules. They quickly learned how to help Leila shower, walk, and manage her medications. They cooked for her, did her laundry—and often mine—and provided stimulating companionship.

In this guide, the terms "caregivers" and "aides" refer to these untrained helpers as well as to certified nursing assistants and personal care workers who have received formal training. Many men are working as caregivers. Leila preferred women caregivers because of the intimate nature of her care.

Neighbors and friends

Our neighbors sometimes brought us meals. Anytime I could get respite from cooking, I took it. Occasionally I would ask a neighbor to visit with Leila while I ran an errand. Several had keys to our home and were volunteers in Leila's emergency-response system run by our local hospital. I sometimes paid the high school girls who lived next door to help Leila remain safe while I was out of the house for an hour or two.

Several friends who lived at a distance were unfailingly supportive of us. The most meaningful aspect of the help from neighbors and friends was their commitment to helping us live contentedly and manage the crises that jeopardized Leila's life.

How We Found Our Aides and Respite Volunteers

Our homecare agency assistance

Because I was new to caregiving when we first looked for help, we used the agency associated with our local hospital. It had a good reputation. There are several homecare agencies in many communities. Contact your parents' Key Resources (page 248) and ask everyone you talk to about agencies' reputations. Your parents' physician and nurses should be a good information source.

Find out if an agency sends the same caregivers to their clients' homes as much as possible. If not, your parent may not be helped very often by aides he knows and trusts and who understand how best to provide his care. What is the agency's reputation for ensuring that its aides show up, and show up on time?

Our self-employed certified aides

In many places there are networks of self-employed certified nursing assistants. These aides know each other because they often work in the same homes. We had such a network in Racine. I found these self-employed in-home caregivers by asking:

▸ The homecare agency's aides who were already helping us

▸ Members of caregiver support groups

▸ Nurses or aides who helped us in the hospital. "Do you do any freelance work? Do you know anyone you trust who does that kind of work?"

▸ Nurses in physicians' offices

▸ Nursing home social workers

▸ Local government social workers in human services and aging

▸ Respite services organizations

I also found aides by posting bulletin board notices in:

▶ Nursing schools

▶ Technical schools that provide training for aide certification

Our new caregivers connected me to others. I could have recruited aides through newspaper ads. Sometimes in-home caregivers place their own newspaper ads. Some communities have networks of independent registered nurses. Whether you wish to employ one of these nurses, tapping into this network may help you find self-employed caregivers.

Some organizations can help you find caregivers who will live with older adults requiring constant care. Friends of our family have had a couple from an Eastern European country living with them for several years. This arrangement has been excellent for all of them. Ask the Key Resources, page 248, about these kinds of arrangements.

Our untrained caregivers

These aides were, generally, women who did not know they could do this kind of work until I found them and showed them. Discovering them was not as difficult as I thought it would be. I found them through:

▶ Women already working with us

▶ Our respite service organization

▶ Other community volunteer organizations

▶ Leila's church

In each case I asked the same question: "Do you know a reliable person who would be good at this?" Through this networking, I found several mothers who wanted work when their children were in school and for some evenings. I found several others through them.

Compassion, common sense, competence and honesty were at the top of my list of requirements for all the caregivers who came to our home. Two additional absolute *musts*:

> ▸ Showing up on time, not "I didn't think you would mind if I got here 15 minutes late. I had to stop at the store."

> ▸ Showing up, *period*. A few otherwise excellent aides had misplaced priorities. Those night-before "Gee, I'm really sorry" calls were deal-breakers.

Our respite volunteers

I found our respite services agency on a list published by our county aging services department. Your Key Resources will also be able to help you (page 248).

Other Ways to Find In-Home Workers

In Chapter 17 you will find a list of supportive community services such as senior centers. Check with staff of these programs to see if they know anyone who could help your parents.

Some private agencies have lists of certified self-employed aides on "registries." Some of these agencies charge customers for their recruitment services. These agencies are not homecare providers and the aides are not their employees.

"Get personal" with state and community government organizations that deal with aging or disability issues. Ask for local contacts who can help you find competent independent in-home workers. If the person who answers the phone doesn't have that kind of information, ask if there is someone there who might. (See Key Resources, page 248.)

You are overloaded. Searching for the assistance needed by your parent can seem impossible. This is one of those times when "frontloading" can pay terrific dividends. More time now can mean much less later.

How Will You Know You Can Trust the People You Employ?

I was usually certain about the integrity of the women who came to work for us because of who had referred them. *Without unquestionable referrals, you will need to run formal background checks, even on aides listed on private registries.* Most states have their own registry that includes every certified nursing assistant employed by nursing homes or home health agencies.

The aides on these lists have met federal and state training requirements. State registries also list aides who have committed harmful acts against persons for whom they were caring. These lists usually do not include independent aides, but that is changing in some states. You may not want to rely solely on a state registry. Sometimes these lists are not updated as frequently as they should be.

You can find your state registry easily by using an Internet search engine. Search for *certified nurse assistant registry + name of state*.

Your state may also provide a web site that will disclose whether the person you are considering has had judgments against him in any circuit court in your state. The National Center for State Courts provides links to state court web sites. www.ncsconline.org

Your police department should be able to assist you. At mine I can obtain individual arrest records. For a small fee I also can obtain a "profile" which includes lesser offenses, such as Driving Under the Influence.

Many states provide public access to criminal records. To find this information check with a police department or search the Internet for *Criminal background checks + name of state*. The rules governing access to these records will vary across states.

The person seeking employment may have to authorize the release of this personal information in some instances. A homecare agency director reminded me that it may be wise to run another background check on an employed aide later on, as well.

The Right Person May Be Right in Front of You

CʒʒƧ☉

Fred needed help preparing his meals. He could not leave his home on his own because of physical disabilities and memory problems. His son, Mike, was missing work to take Fred to doctors' appointments, prepare his lunches and respond to crises such as his dad locking himself out of his home.

I suggested that Mike should find someone to help him. He said his dad would not accept assistance from a "health agency." I reminded him that Fred did not need a healthcare worker; he needed someone to do what Mike was doing. Several times over many months, I asked Mike to think more creatively. Who else was in his dad's life that might be the answer: An old friend, a neighbor, a student who could use some spending money? Each time, the answer was, "There isn't anyone like that." It wasn't that Mike didn't try; he just could not see any options.

One day, Mike called me. "Terry! I think I found her. The person who can help my dad at home." A young mother, Julie, was cleaning Fred's home weekly. Fred enjoyed her company. Julie had time for additional work, common sense and cooking skills far superior to Mike and Fred's. She was delighted to take on extra responsibilities. She helped Fred until he moved to an assisted living residence.

CʒʒƧ☉

What's Better: Homecare Agency or Independent Aides?

Arguments for relying on independent caregivers

I have discussed some advantages for Leila and me of hiring independent aides instead of relying completely on homecare agency help: more control over who came into our home, flexibility in scheduling, and lower costs. You would have to determine which arrangement would be less expensive in your parent's circumstances.

Other considerations:

▶ *If an agency does not retain its aides very long, neither will you.* We found that self-employed aides were less likely to leave for other opportunities, as long as they were compensated fairly. Some of them helped us for almost 10 years.

▶ *An independent aide could help you manage your parent's schedule* and stay on top of what is going on. Several assisted me with those tasks over the years.

▶ *Does the agency deliver on its "We provide excellent and reliable care" promise?* Some agencies hire only capable and reliable aides. Some don't.

Not all homecare agencies are as diligent as ours was about ensuring that their caregivers show up on time. Not all are able to provide back-up care, should a scheduled aide be unable to come to work.

It is essential to network for this kind of information before making a decision on which agency to use, if you have time and if you have options. If there are no realistic alternatives, hiring independent caregivers may be the only way to go.

Advantages of using the services of a homecare agency

▶ *You don't need to be an instant expert.*
If your parent has been self-reliant and should suddenly need in-home care, you might not know where to turn. An agency might be your only viable short-term option, as it was for Leila and me.

▶ *You might save time and energy over the long run.*
An excellent agency should be able to provide your parent the assistance he needs when he needs it. You will not have to recruit the aides or pay them directly. If a regularly scheduled caregiver cannot come to work, the agency often can provide a backup.

▶ *Many agencies run their own background checks before they hire in-home workers.* Be sure to ask.

▶ *If you live at a distance from your parents, you may have no choice.*
If your parents are unable to manage hiring and scheduling independent caregivers and there is no one in their community to do it for them, a homecare agency can be extraordinarily important to their continued self-reliance.

▶ *Your parents' health needs may require ongoing agency assistance.*
Many homecare agencies provide the services of home-health nurses as well as home-health aides trained to work under nurse supervision. Where elders are medically fragile, as Leila was, having some degree of ongoing healthcare services can be lifesaving.

Remember that Medicare covers in-home healthcare only in certain circumstances (page 45). You may find it is worth paying for some home-health services ("private pay"), when Medicare does not cover them. That is what we would have done, if Leila had not been assisted by state-funded programs.

▶ *You don't have the tax responsibilities you have when you hire your own in-home workers.*

The Internal Revenue Service classifies as household employees any aides that you hire and who work under your direction. Consequently, you or your parent (whoever pays the independent aide), must withhold federal Medicare and Social Security taxes when that aide's wages reach a certain level, unless you pay his taxes for him. In 2008 that level is $1,600. You also would have to pay the employer's share of those taxes. You might be responsible for federal and state unemployment taxes. Check with your parents' state Department of Labor or Revenue (or their accountant).

We paid our taxes and the aides' taxes, but our total annual expenditure for their work was still lower than the costs for homecare agency services would have been. Once I got the hang of doing the paperwork associated with employing independent caregivers, it became second nature. And it caused me far fewer headaches than I probably would have had if Leila had moved to a nursing home.

Costs for personal care will, of course, vary according to location and increase over time. Consequently, this example will provide only a general idea of what your costs might be. Today in southeastern Wisconsin, families with personal care needs can find excellent self-employed aides for $15 an hour. Agency personal care rates range from $17-$25 an hour. In places with higher costs of living, these rates will be substantially higher, as well.

▶ *A reliable agency will have insurance that protects your parents and you from a liability claim if an aide should be injured on the job.*

Other important points:

▶ Anyone who employs independent caregivers should have insurance that protects her financial assets if one of these aides should be injured in her home. Also consider insurance that covers "third party" injuries caused by a caregiver, for instance an injury to a pedestrian hit by an aide while driving your parent to an appointment. An agency with expertise in liability insurance can help with these issues.

▶ Some self-employed aides may tell you they will work only for "cash" (undeclared, untaxed wages). This kind of arrangement is not uncommon, but it is not legal.

Don't overlook the adult day program

CR&O

I saw Becky in our local grocery store. Her family was in turmoil because her sister "...had to put mom in a nursing home." I asked why. "Margie had to go back to work and they couldn't afford to pay someone to be with mom all day." I asked if Margie and her husband had considered an adult day program as an alternative to the nursing home. Becky hesitated. Then she told me, "I am afraid no one thought of that."

CR&O

If I had not been able to find substantial resources for in-home care for Leila, adult day services probably would have been the next step. Adult day centers provide safe environments to elders and often to others with disabilities who cannot be alone at home. Many day programs include people with dementia. The costs are modest compared to the cost of eight-hour homecare.

Adult day centers generally operate programs during normal business hours five days a week. Some offer services in the evenings and on weekends. Some programs offer meals, assistance with personal care, and social activities, while other day programs provide more services, such as medical care, exercise sessions, recreational activities and physical therapy.

"It will never work" means it will never work

CB∂

I was in Milwaukee speaking to a group of family caregivers about "Tapping Community Resources." An audience member stopped me. "Mr. Lynch, there is nothing you have told us so far that will help my mother or me. None of this will ever work for us." I gulped, faked a smile and asked her why. "My mother only speaks German, so there is no one who could help her at home."

I took a gamble. I replied that the audience was a kind of community—a temporary community dealing with a common problem. Since we were in a city with a large German-speaking population, I bet we could get some ideas on finding help for her mother "right now." A woman across the room said, "I can do better than ideas. I've got someone for you. I know a family from (another European nation) that speaks fluent German. Two sisters in that family are looking for that kind of work."

The daughter replied, "We would never have someone from that country in our home." Some audience members gasped with disappointment.

CB∂

Learning about everything that's "out there" can be discouraging. It overwhelmed me at first. Having a lot to work with means a lot to learn about; then you have to figure out what to do with it all. Take heart. Believe that you *will* make it work. Once you have even a small start, you will be better able to put the rest of the pieces together.

You bring in a homecare agency for short-term help while you work on a long-term plan. Its social worker suggests some medical equipment that will help your parents manage their lives. You learn that its costs are covered by Medicare and Medicare supplemental insurance.

An aide knows someone reliable who is looking for "some hours." The new caregiver takes your mother to a church meal program twice a week. She meets some new friends. You start to build a team. Before you know it, you are getting a handle on a way of life that is working well for thousands of other families.

Preventing Accidents
and Injuries

Chapter 19

Creating a Safer Home

Leila's caregivers and I justifiably were obsessed with her safety. Her frailty, balance difficulties, memory disorder and occasional adverse reactions to medications kept us constantly on edge. One reason Leila lived to 89 was our success in limiting her accidents and injuries. You will find a discussion of hazards to avoid and tips to follow in avoiding falls in Chapter 2, page 9. This chapter expands on what else you can do to assist your parents to remain as safe as possible at home.

Even with substantial help from government programs, Leila and I could not afford constant help from paid caregivers. Unless Leila was ill or unusually weak, neither of us wanted her to depend on me for hourly assistance with activities such as walking around the home or using the toilet. She didn't want me, or anyone else, hovering over her. Consequently, I had to devise a system that would enable Leila to retain her cherished self-reliance and also limit her risk of injury.

The system that worked for us combined three elements:

▶ Modification and rearrangement of our living space

▶ Equipment and devices to help Leila maneuver within this environment

▶ Leila's determination to maintain her strength and mobility

Modifying the Home

Strange changes

Because Leila could not use stairs safely, I had the kitchen pantry remade into a shower room and bathroom. We also used other rooms in "strange ways" according to some of Leila's friends. Both she and I had to be flexible. The dining room became Leila's bedroom—for 10 years. We also used it as a social room with a small couch and a comfortable chair. The living room now was also our dining room. When Leila was ill or injured, the living-room couch became my bed.

Some wondered how we could live that way. It was much better than the alternative. We were still in our home. We got used to these changes and so did our friends. I was certain it would be easier for me to manage this system than to help Leila manage life in a nursing home.

The present and future of home modification

Frail elders and others with physical and sensory impairments have many options for making their homes safer and easier to live in. Various devices and alarms allow people with memory loss to remain at home safely as long as possible. This technology will continue to expand. Much of the new technology costs more than those with modest incomes may be able to afford. However, some of it, although expensive, ultimately can save thousands of dollars in medical or residential costs—for instance by helping avoid a move to a nursing home.

The National Center for Supportive Housing and Home Modification has an extraordinarily useful web site. It provides extensive information on home safety and modification and many links to organizations involved in home adaptation: www.homemods.org. Also see www.aarp.org. Search for *Universal Design.*

Many Independent Living Centers offer cost-free assessments of home safety, including safety for people with sensory impairments. ILC staff are experts on home modification and on devices that promote independence. (Key Resources, page 248.)

Invaluable Affordable Equipment
(Inanimate objects can mean a lot)

Any device or tool that improves the ability of a person with a disability to do something himself is categorized as "adaptive equipment." Leila and I relied more than I could have imagined on these resources. They assisted her to avoid injuries, remain relatively self-reliant, and reduced her need for "hands on," more costly, assistance.

The equipment that was most useful to us

▶ *Commode*
A portable toilet designed to enable a person to use it safely. We kept it next to Leila's bed. Because of the commode, I didn't have to get up to help her most nights.

▶ *Hospital bed*
Safer and more comfortable than a standard bed. It had guard rails and could be raised or lowered to help Leila get in and out of bed safely.

▶ *Walker*
A four-legged device that enabled Leila to walk throughout her difficult later years. Walkers have creative designs for carrying useful things such as cordless telephones. I have an older friend whose walker has a seat on it that enables her to rest as she moves around her home. It has wheels with brakes.

▸ *Portable wheelchair*
Light and foldable and it fit in my automobile's trunk. Before you buy a wheelchair make certain that you can transport it.

Many other kinds of adaptive equipment might work well in your parents' situation.

DME could be the answer

Some very helpful low-cost adaptive equipment is known as Durable Medical Equipment (DME). DME is prescribed by physicians or other medical professionals, such as physicians' assistants, for use at home. Most of the costs of DME will be covered by Medicare. Your physician may have to receive Medicare approval to prescribe some kinds of DME.

Medicare will purchase immediately some DME, such as canes, but its policy is to rent most equipment with an option to purchase. If you choose to buy the item, as Leila and I did with her hospital bed, Medicare will cover 80 percent of the cost. More of the cost will be covered if your parent has a supplemental Medicare policy ("Medigap" insurance, page 15) or is a Medicaid beneficiary.

The Medicare web site provides the most accurate and up-to-date information on what kinds of DME Medicare covers and on rental/purchase policies. The easiest way to find this information is to contact a DME supplier (retailer) enrolled in Medicare. Your parent's physician will be able to recommend a reputable vendor. Also see the Helpful Contacts page on the Medicare website: www.medicare.gov.

Home health agencies and Independent Living Centers also will have this information and may supply DME. (See Key Resources, page 248.) The equipment retailer I worked with was extraordinarily helpful in documenting Leila's need for DME so that it would be covered by Medicare or Medicaid. Medicare also covers many kinds of prosthetics and orthotics, which are devices that help individuals adapt to the disabling impact of injuries and disease.

Some of the covered devices

▶ Artificial limbs and eyes

▶ Arm, back, leg and neck braces

▶ Therapeutic shoes for people with severe foot disease caused by diabetes

▶ Cataract glasses

Again, this is merely an example list. It may seem strange to include prosthetics and orthotics under DME, but that is how they are categorized by Medicare. If you are enrolled in a private Medicare plan, check with the administrators of that plan on what DME it covers.

🖅 *Before you purchase equipment or adaptive devices, be certain you not only need it but that it will function as advertised. For instance, some "roll-in" showers have edges on them that make them "non-roll-in" showers. If you feel pressured by a sales representative, you might want to find a vendor whose sales people do not work on commission. An excellent vendor will do an excellent cost-free assessment of what is needed at home.*

Commonplace technology that made life safer

▶ *Intercom system*
One transmitter was next to Leila's bed and the other was in my upstairs bedroom. This allowed her to contact me if she needed me during the night. It enabled me to get a good night's sleep without worrying.

▶ *Cordless telephone*
Leila carried it with her as she moved around the home; we also kept one next to her bed at night, as an emergency backup.

▶ *Emergency response system*
For a small monthly fee, our local hospital set Leila up with

equipment connected to the telephone line. A contact button worn around her neck enabled Leila to get immediate assistance from neighbors if she should need it. Several emergency-response alternatives may be available to your parents.

A web page maintained by the National Institute on Disability and Rehabilitation Research provides comprehensive information on assistive-technology products and where to find them. Its Resources link takes you to "all the Internet resources known to us on a selected disability issue, all in one page." www.abledata.com

Keep the "Stairs" in Your Parents' Lives

Build on what comes naturally

Nothing was more important to Leila's safety than maintaining her flexibility, muscle strength and balance.

The best "workouts" for Leila were activities that were part of her everyday routine. Leila didn't want medical devices or equipment that she didn't absolutely need. Consequently I did not purchase chairs with electronic lifts to help her sit or stand. (These chairs are valuable additions to many homes, however.) Her aides and I assisted Leila to get in and out of chairs, but she still had to use arm and leg strength.

We did not build a ramp to the front porch. I put a strong railing on the steps and we helped Leila struggle up and down those four steps for 10 years. Leila asked us to help her stick to this rule: Use the wheelchair only when she needed it. We tried not to use it just for our convenience.

The safety payoffs were substantial. Sustaining Leila's strength helped her use her commode safely at night even as the years passed and kept her from falling when she used her walker on her own. It improved her balance and made life easier on all of us. Continued participation in everyday life helped her continue to enjoy that life safely.

The remarkable benefits of pumping iron

🙰🙵

I met Lars and his wife, Ruth Ann in a local coffee shop. They were in their early 80s. Ruth Ann was physically active. Lars was frail and weak. It was difficult for him to walk. I asked him if he had considered physical therapy. He laughed. I didn't. I told him that if his physician thought it was appropriate, she could order it and Medicare would cover much of the cost. Why would Medicare cover it? One reason is to help people in his situation regain strength and mobility.

Ruth Ann said she would "work on" talking Lars into taking my advice. Several months later, Ruth Ann told me Lars was getting out-patient physical therapy and was "stronger and healthier." Almost a year passed before I saw Ruth Ann again. She told me Lars had just undergone successful major surgery. She and their children believed his therapy program was the reason he was strong enough to survive it.

🙰🙵

We used physical therapy at home quite often, usually to help Leila recover from an injury or illness. Her physicians sometimes would not have thought of it but were always supportive when I asked them to order it.

Physical therapists taught Leila safe "weight-lifting" (resistance) exercises. She had light ankle weights for building leg strength. She could take them off and use them for arm-strengthening exercises. Leila never said, "Gee, when can we start with the weights today?" She, however, realized these exercises helped and did them with relatively minor griping. *Any resistance exercises for a frail person should be done only with the supervision of a healthcare professional.*

Occupational therapists assist frail elders and people with disabilities to manage daily life—for instance, teaching people recovering from a stroke how to groom themselves and use their kitchens safely.

Therapy goes beyond maintaining or improving strength, mobility and flexibility. There is a physical therapy specialization for problems with dizziness and loss of balance. Neither of these problems should be considered inevitable at any age.

🔲 *Researchers at Yale University found a 45 percent reduction in disability in a group of 188 frail elders who received seven months of physical therapy at home. This therapy focused on improving balance, muscle strength and mobility. (Yale Bulletin and Calendar, Oct 18, 2002)*

Chapter 20

I Want Mom to Stop Driving. But Then What?

In my experience, concern about parents and driving safety is second only to health issues. And when a parent surrenders the car keys the pressing question often becomes *"How is he going to be able to get along at home?"* Good question. Limited transportation options underlie many moves to group residences by elders who otherwise could remain in their homes.

Try to Head Off "You Should Not Be Driving"

A parent stops driving. Her friends do not drive. Isolation and poor nutrition lead to depression and increasing confusion. It becomes hazardous for her to remain at home. In such circumstances, a move may be the best answer. There are, however, several steps you and your parent can take to try to avoid these unfortunate situations.

Check for medical problems that affect safe driving

Use this guide to assist your parent to prevent or overcome life-altering medical, sensory and mobility problems. And watch out for adverse reactions to medications that can affect driver safety.

Take advantage of self-assessment tools and driver education resources

As we age, inevitable changes such as hearing loss and slowed reaction time affect our ability to drive. The resources listed below will help your parent assess and improve his driving skills. These respectful and consumer-friendly resources also provide advice on how he can modify his driving habits to continue to drive safely—for instance, only driving during the day or avoiding left turns in heavy traffic.

These resources also will help you raise concerns with your parents considerately and effectively. They include

▶ *"How to Help the Older Driver"* and *"Drivers 55 Plus: Test Your Own Performance"*, published by the American Automobile Association (AAA) Foundation for Traffic Safety: www.seniordrivers.org. Click on *Giving Up Keys*.

▶ Internet AARP older driver resources. These resources on safe driving are extensive. They include an on-line safe driving assessment quiz. Look for www.aarp.org, search for *Driver Safety*.

Ask your parent to participate in a driver education class. AARP provides classes at multiple locations in each state. You can find statewide and community schedules on the AARP homepage (above). AAA also will have information on driver education classes near your parents. Contact the Department of Motor Vehicles in your parents' state. Its staff can help them assess their skills, drive more safely and understand when it may be time to stop driving.

Be sure to review the publications in this chapter before you approach a parent with concerns about his driving. You will learn what questions to raise, how to raise them and strategies for getting him to listen. The Hartford Insurance Company's *Alzheimer's, Dementia and Driving* will be valuable to families concerned about a parent's confusion and memory loss. It also is a must-read for other families as well. www.thehartford.com Search for *Alzheimer's driving*.

What if These Ideas Don't Work?

Take a careful and strategic approach to the conversation

Persuading your parent to relinquish the car keys can be stressful and heartbreaking, but less so than a tragic and avoidable traffic accident. Before you try, read *Family Conversations with Older Drivers*, published by the Massachusetts Institute for Technology's Age Lab and The Hartford Insurance Company. www.thehartford.com/conversationswitholderdrivers

You may have to use the last resort

In some cases, especially where parents have dementia, conversation and persuasion won't work. Your parent's physician, police department, and the motor vehicle department each may be able to take steps to keep your parent, and her community, safe.

Help Your Parent Create Her Own Transportation System

❦❧

Jesse called me long distance. His mother-in-law, Myra, lived in Racine and could no longer see well enough to drive. Jesse asked me about transportation alternatives. I told him about a volunteer organization that provided low-cost transportation in private vehicles.

Jesse connected Myra to that organization. This connection opened her community to her in ways we could not have anticipated. The first volunteer driver turned out to be a young woman, Macy, who had lived near Myra as a child. Macy asked her, "Why didn't you just call me in the first place?" Myra now could coordinate her schedule with Macy's. When Macy could not drive, another volunteer did. Sometimes Myra took a cab.

CRSO

Myra was unusually fortunate. However, your parent may be able to find similar kinds of transportation assistance in her community if you help her think creatively. There may be neighbors or even acquaintances who will say: "Why didn't you just call me in the first place?" Find aides who do in-home care and ask if they will provide a few hours of transportation now and then. Could there be church members who will help out? Agencies that provide van services may be another option.

Go back to Chapter 5, "Take Advantage of Your Natural Resources" and also re-read the chapters in this Part. They will give you a blueprint to follow.

Your parent's need to participate in community life will not end if he should move to senior housing. Keep working on the transportation system.

Moving: When Is It Time? What Do We Do?

Overview

My short answer to *When is it time for my parents to move?*

▶ When they wish to

▶ If everything that I suggest in this guide no longer works

▶ If your parents have cognitive impairments that cause them to endanger themselves or others

▶ If increasing isolation leads to problems such as depression or poor nutrition

If this was my complete answer, however, you wouldn't meet Edna. Her story in Chapter 21 is a unique illustration of this guide's process for working through the "Is it time?" issue.

Chapter 22 provides examples of when a move is necessary to preserve the well-being of an overloaded caregiver.

In Chapter 23 you will find a summary of housing alternatives and some of the living arrangements on the horizon.

Chapter 21

Edna: Almost, but Not Quite

Leila's friend, Edna, another retired teacher, called to ask a favor. Edna, 90, had been single and independent all her life. She had lived in the same, comfortable second-floor flat for 20 years. Edna was frail, almost completely blind, and had heart disease. The favor: Edna wanted me to help her move to "a suitable care home."

I immediately thought of what places might be "suitable." Then I made one innocent comment that changed the focus of our conversation and caused me to think more about "When it's time." I told Edna I could imagine that she was finding it dangerous to navigate around her apartment because of poor vision. Edna replied, "Oh my, no! I have been able to get around here in the dark for years." I was surprised by her answer and decided to take the questions farther down-line:

▸ Was climbing the stairs getting too difficult? "No, I have the railing to hang onto. And that's the only good exercise I get."

▸ Was she feeling isolated and lonely? No, her gentleman friend down the street was still driving her around town occasionally and her downstairs neighbors were good to her.

▸ Was she afraid at night because of her heart condition? "Not at all. I have my neighbors and I have my hospital emergency button to push if I need help."

I told Edna I was confused. What kind of help did she need that required a move? She said she was having trouble seeing well enough to prepare meals and pay her bills. Sometimes it was difficult to get out for groceries. I told her those problems could be handled without having to leave her home. Edna exclaimed, "I was hoping you would say that! I love it here. But my friends say I need to leave my apartment. They are worried about me."

With a few small steps, I was able to help Edna stay in her home. I contacted a wonderful self-employed homecare aide nicknamed "Betty Crocker" for her legendary cooking skills. Betty spent eight hours a week with Edna for the next two years. She prepared meals and froze them in microwave-ready containers. Betty paid Edna's bills and took her shopping. Sometimes they went out to lunch.

Several times Edna's heart condition sent her to the hospital. Each time she returned to her home and to Betty Crocker. When Edna needed more help, Betty provided it or found it for her. They became good friends.

This system worked until Edna's heart condition worsened. She spent her last few years with her niece in Florida. I occasionally wonder how her life would have turned out if, when Edna asked me to help her move, my first question had been: "When do you want to start looking?"

When Is the Right Time?

I would have encouraged Edna to consider moving if

▸ she was struggling with untreatable memory loss.

▸ her health became so poor she needed emergency assistance nearby at all times.

▶ she felt endangered moving around her apartment or climbing stairs.

▶ she felt isolated and lonely, even with several Betties in her life.

Even if Edna had wished to move because of vision or health problems, and did not have her niece to count on, a nursing home might not have been the answer. An assisted living residence or another kind of group residence might have provided what she needed. (See Chapter 23.)

Your parents may decide to move for reasons unrelated to health, such as to

▶ live in a smaller and more manageable place.

▶ live closer to family or friends.

▶ have a safer living arrangement and home remodeling would be too costly.

▶ improve their social life.

▶ sell their home because they need the money.

Before your parent decides to move because of living costs, review the options for generating more cash from home ownership (page 50). Also, check on eligibility for programs that assist with the costs of home modification (page 180).

When a Parent Harms Herself

Sometimes a parent neglects her health and well-being because she no longer has the capacity to care for herself. In these cases, families might consider protective placement, which requires a court to determine whether an elder is competent. In cases of incapacity the court orders a guardianship. The guardian works out a protective living arrangement. It is very important that the guardian knows and cares about the older person who has become his or her "ward." (See Chapter 4.)

Chapter 22

Your Overloaded Life May Tip the Balance

"This is good for everyone concerned."

ଓଃ৪ৎ

Margaret loved her home, where she lived alone, but decided to move to an assisted living residence. Her vision and mobility were impaired by the effects of diabetes. She felt lonely at times. However, she could have continued living at home at a reasonable additional cost with more in-home assistance than she was receiving. But Margaret was concerned for her son, Hank, who lived nearby with his family. Hank was devoting much of his time to his mother and was increasingly anxious about leaving her alone.

Margaret wanted to relieve Hank of the pressure. Her other son, George, lived 40 miles away and was happy to have her near him. He helped his mother find a place she liked. Margaret now has a small apartment that she finds "cozy." It is decorated with pictures from her home and several pieces of her favorite furniture. She has her meals in a communal dining room. Aides help her with bathing and dressing and generally look out for her. Some of the other

199

residents have become her friends. George takes care of Margaret's financial affairs and healthcare and involves her in his family life.

Margaret spends most of her time in her apartment reading or watching television. She tells me, "I enjoy my own company." She is content in her new life but misses her home and her dogs. Overall, Margaret believes the move has been "good for everyone concerned." Hank lives close enough to be able to visit on weekends. He misses his mother but "seems happier." Margaret realizes there are significant tradeoffs at her stage of life and is willing to live with them.

CR&ED

"Twenty miles sure beats hundreds!"

CR&ED

Evelyn's mother, Esther, who lived on her own in Nebraska, was struggling with several difficult medical problems. She also seemed depressed. Evelyn was constantly involved in her mother's care from long distance in Wisconsin. Evelyn also was trying to find time for home life with her husband and their young son. She asked her mother to move to Wisconsin and Esther agreed.

Evelyn's family situation did not allow for her mother to live with them. She found a nearby nursing home that met her and Esther's approval. The move turned out well for mother and daughter. Esther's depression faded as she met other residents. Evelyn visited her often, helped manage her medical care, and found time for family life. Evelyn told me, "Twenty miles sure beats hundreds!"

Two years after Esther's death, Evelyn still is in contact with some of the nursing home staff that cared for her mother.

CR&ED

These stories represent ideal outcomes in difficult circumstances. The demands on the adult child-caregiver are recognized by a parent and the parent agrees to a lifestyle change that works out well for everyone. I hope this guide will help you and your parent make decisions that come as close as possible to this ideal. Where the ideal is not possible, try to work on other ways of taking care of yourself and putting more allies in your parent's life.

Chapter 23

Go Out of Your Way to Find Homelike

When a parent moves, focus on keeping the flame burning. Help her find a residence where she feels, or is likely to feel, at home. The features of home that Margaret enjoys in her new residence include privacy, cherished possessions, comfort, contact with friends and family, and control, by and large, of how she spends her days.

What Are the Alternatives?

The options are expanding rapidly. Unfortunately, some are too costly for many older people. Although our federal and state governments spend large amounts on "alternative housing," much of this housing is in nursing homes. These funds are mostly available only to those who qualify for Medicaid.

Because the information on current housing options and trends is easily found, I will provide short descriptions. As the "senior market" expands, the basic services offered by each housing alternative will probably expand as well.

Senior housing

- ▶ Refers to rental options including apartments, condominiums, single homes, mobile homes.

- ▶ Often not for those who require assistance with daily living but may offer this assistance at additional cost.

- ▶ May be designed for increasing safety needs (grab bars in bathrooms, specially designed kitchens, emergency response services).

- ▶ May offer services such as group dining, transportation, social activities.

- ▶ Most services are not included in rent payments.

- ▶ Some of this housing is "subsidized." It provides low-cost residences to older adults with limited financial resources.

Independent living apartments

- ▶ Private unfurnished apartments.

- ▶ Group social activities and features such as beauty salons.

- ▶ Services such as light housekeeping, transportation to medical appointments and meals in a central dining area. The rent may not cover these services.

- ▶ Safety features.

- ▶ Some may have wheelchair access.

Assisted living

- ▶ For those who need non-medical assistance, such as help with bathing.

- ▶ Meals in a central dining area.

▶ Small apartments or individual rooms.

▶ Recreation and social activities.

▶ Laundry, housekeeping, transportation and other basic services.

▶ May assist with managing medications.

The range of personal-care services offered by assisted living residences is expanding. I have a friend who, just a few years ago, would be living in a nursing home. She continues to reside in her assisted living apartment because she is getting more help with bathing, dressing and walking than she received even a year ago.

The quality of assisted living residences is, sometimes, not monitored carefully by government agencies. Resident safety and quality of life vary. In my friend's residence, the food, at first, was atrocious. Staff were unhappy. A new owner brought a new work environment and food that is "quite good." The key is finding that kind of owner in the first place. Much of the next Part, on finding and living in a nursing home, will apply to the assisted living world.

▣ *Just because a place looks great, it does not mean it is.*

Continuing Care Retirement Communities

For one (large) payment, these arrangements offer options from senior apartments through assisted living to nursing homes. Residents may move from one kind of residence to another as their need for assistance and medical services increases.

Creative options

Some older persons and their families are taking advantage of unique, common-sense alternatives that include

▶ *Elder Cottage Housing Opportunity Accessory Units (ECHO housing).*
A temporary living unit placed on the property of a family home. Check zoning restrictions.

▶ *Accessory apartment.*
An apartment is set up in or attached to a family home.

▶ *Shared housing.*
Two or more people move in together. Another choice: The parent remains at home and brings in a renter. In some places there are organizations that specialize in matches that fit the needs of both parties. They also keep track of how things are going and help patch the rough spots.

There are less common community-living arrangements that might work for your parents if they live in mutually supportive neighborhoods. Search the Internet for *"Naturally Occurring Residential Communities."* Also visit the AARP web page www.aarp.org. Click on *Family, Home, and Legal*, then on *Housing Choices*.

Contact your parents' Key Resources, page 248, about creative housing arrangements that might be available to them.

▣ *Few "senior housing" options provide full participation in community life. Family, friends, neighbors and volunteers can all enrich the lives of elders who have made these places their new homes.*

Sometimes none of the options for independent living will be appropriate for your parent. A nursing home may be the only choice. How to make it work is the subject of the next Part of this guide.

The Nursing Home: Staying Focused on the Flame

Overview

Her world came with her

ଔଔଔ

One of Leila's seven sisters, Ethel, lived in a small town in western Wisconsin. Leila and I and several of Aunt Ethel's friends threw her a party on her 85ᵗʰ birthday. We gave her silly presents. A neighbor served Aunt Ethel's "favorite creation," an addictive chocolate cake. We laughed and talked for several hours. When it was time to leave, Aunt Ethel told us she thought it was just about the best birthday she had ever had. "I forgot I was in a nursing home."

As we left, one of the aides thanked us enthusiastically for being with Aunt Ethel on her birthday. "And please come back soon!"

ଔଔଔ

Be sure to read every chapter in this guide before deciding that a nursing home is the answer.

Providing a good life for their residents can be challenging for the best of nursing homes. Aunt Ethel's situation illustrates some of the reasons. Her nursing home, "RuralCare," had a good reputation. Its staff treated her well. But RuralCare looked and felt like a small hospital. She had space for only a few possessions. She no longer had a home. She no longer had her privacy. "Her own place" was a cramped room shared with a stranger.

Aunt Ethel had lost much of her life and it was up to the staff to help her build a new one. They hoped her family and friends would assist them. That afternoon we did. She forgot she was living where she didn't want to be.

Although Aunt Ethel required more care than she could find elsewhere, what she needed the most had not changed: A good life, shared with people who loved her. She needed to remain connected to the world beyond nursing home walls.

It should not have been surprising

☙❧

I was teaching a university undergraduate course on the psychology of aging. Several students were in nursing school and also were working as nursing home aides. Class members asked them how to find the best nursing facility for a loved one. After a lively and occasionally disturbing discussion, I asked the class to summarize the most important lessons. One stood out: "The people who get the best care in nursing homes are the ones whose family and friends stay involved."

☙❧

The class discussion highlighted why it is difficult in many nursing homes for aides to provide excellent care to residents, let alone help them build a new life. Their workload is overwhelming. You should expect, as in hospitals, that aides will provide better care to your parent if you remain intimately involved in her life.

Aunt Ethel eventually liked RuralCare. The morale of the aides was generally high. Consequently, few left their jobs. Many nursing homes are constantly hiring new caregivers due to turnover. The staff got to know Ethel well and had time to give her good care. They took her out into her community. Her community came to see her. Several aides became her friends.

I know several other nursing home success stories. A former nurse supervisor told me she had seen new residents *"blossom, have a new lease on life because they had been so lonely and isolated."* The mother of a close friend *"thrived because of wonderful nurse assistants and new friends."*

Not all nursing home residents in the United States have been as fortunate. Many have experienced neglectful treatment or have been abused. Residential services organizations, nursing home administrators, government agencies and nursing home advocates have struggled for years to end these problems. The federal government's Residents' Rights requirements and the state nursing home investigations discussed later reflect this nationwide effort to improve residents' lives.

The obstacles are formidable. Many elders in nursing homes have no visitors. None, ever. Problems with resident care might be reduced if they did. Excellent staff often struggle to provide quality services in part because of a nursing shortage and difficulty in recruiting and retaining experienced aides. Many nursing homes are struggling financially. There is much you can do to assist staff to provide your parent with the best possible life. This Part will point you in the right direction.

Previous chapters should have helped you answer: "How will I know when my parent needs a nursing home?" This Part will guide you to excellent resources that, along with this book, will assist you to find the best place for your parent. It will help you ensure that his life goes as well as possible once he moves in.

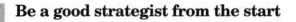

Be a good strategist from the start

You want:

▶ The best possible life for your parent.

▶ The least possible anxiety for yourself.

Fit your actions to these goals.

When I discuss what "you" can do to help your parent, I also am referring to other family members, friends and volunteers. There is much to learn and do. This is no time to take a go-it-alone approach. You will find allies along the way. This guide will help you find them.

Chapter 24

How Do We Find the Best Place?

Prepare for the Nursing Home World

When you walk into a nursing home, you enter an unfamiliar world. You are now in a "healthcare facility" that also serves as the permanent home for many residents. The better you understand that world before you begin your search, the more likely you are to choose the right place. Even if you are under pressure to find a nursing home you should have time for these steps.

Know the residents' rights

Any nursing home receiving Medicare, Medicaid or other federal funds must follow federal requirements for protecting the rights of each resident, such as the right to be treated with dignity. I discuss a number of these rights in the following chapters. For a complete list, visit www.nccnhr.org (National Citizens' Coalition for Nursing Home Reform). Click on *Fact Sheets*, then *Residents' Rights*. The Coalition has been a force behind national efforts to improve nursing home quality.

The Medicare *Guide to Nursing Homes* also describes these rights. (See below.)

⏏ *Many elders enter a nursing home after discharge from a hospital. Medicare will pay for up to 100 days for their care. During this period, residents are to receive skilled services, including physical therapy, to assist them to return home if possible. The kinds of family involvement discussed in this chapter are essential in many instances to a parent's successful rehabilitation.*

Learn how to evaluate nursing home quality

Review:

▶ The rest of this guide.

▶ Medicare's Nursing Home Checklist on what to look for when you visit a nursing facility. www.medicare.gov, search for *Nursing Home Checklist*.

▶ The guide to visiting nursing homes by the American Association of Homes and Services for the Aging is at www.aahsa.org, search for *Tour Nursing Homes*.

I suggest printing the Checklist and referring to it throughout the process of selecting your parent's new home and helping him adjust. Excellent, more extensive guides to understanding the nursing home world are available. If you have more time, look at

• Medicare's *Guide to Nursing Homes,* www.medicare.gov, search for *Nursing Home Publications*.

• National Citizens' Coalition for Nursing Home Reform's *Consumer Guide to Choosing a Nursing Home*, www.nccnhr.org, click on *Fact Sheets*.

Network to Narrow Your Choices

You now should be better prepared to ask informed questions about nursing homes. Many home-health agency staff, members of the clergy, hospital nurses, physicians and coordinators of caregiver support groups will have valuable information. If you know a nursing home employee, be sure to talk with her. If any of the facilities on your list have Family or Resident Councils, speak with some of their members.

▣ *Medicare's Nursing Home Compare web site provides information on all federally certified nursing homes in every state. (See below.)*

The nearest Alzheimer's Association office will have information on how to identify local nursing homes that provide the best care to people with dementia. Even if your parent does not have a memory disorder, this office should be helpful regarding the best choices for your parent.Go to www.alz.org, click on *Find Us Anywhere*.

Check with State Government

Every state has an agency called the state Long-Term Care Ombudsman and a state government survey agency that licenses and inspects nursing homes. These agencies are responsible for protecting the well-being of nursing home residents and helping residents and families resolve complaints.

Each agency welcomes inquiries from the public. Their staff won't advise you on what facilities are best. However, they will tell you about the results of state nursing home inspections and whether there are current complaints regarding a nursing home's quality of care.

Your parents' state Ombudsman can tell you how to contact the survey agency. The Ombudsman is a very useful and consumer-friendly resource to call on throughout the nursing home experience. Their staff are often overloaded with work. You may need to call back if you do not get a timely response. Even if the person you talk to is not supposed to recommend one nursing home over another, you might be able to get this information if you ask. "What would you do if you were in my place?" Look for www.ltcombudsman.org, click on *Ombudsman Locator*.

Ask the Ombudsman or survey agency staff whether any of the nursing homes on your list participate in voluntary state programs to improve resident care. These programs are known as state Quality Improvement Initiatives. If so, it could be an additional indicator of a nursing home's commitment to providing good care to its residents.

Check Nursing Home Compare (NHC)
www.medicare.gov, click on *Compare Nursing Homes*

NHC provides information about each nursing home, including

▶ The number of residents, whether it is Medicare and Medicaid certified, and the average number of hours aides spend with each resident as reported by the nursing facility;

▶ Whether state inspectors have found violations of federal or state requirements for resident care (Click on *Inspections*); and

▶ Problems with quality of care reported by the nursing homes themselves. Click on *Quality*.

What you learn from this information should not be the only basis for your decision. The quality and inspection reports will tell you whether a nursing facility has had difficulty meeting *minimum* requirements. You will not learn about the quality of residents' lives. Also, inspection information could be more than a year old. One former nursing home staff member told me, "They miss some of the violations." Another former nursing home employee believes inspectors are "tougher" on some nursing homes than others.

Visit the Places Still in the Running

Schedule visits to each remaining nursing home. Involve your parent in these visits. You are looking for his new home. You may want to make more than one visit to get a better idea of daily life. Help your parent meet some of the residents.

Write out your questions about the facility. Take them and your checklists when you visit and *use them*. Nursing home staff will respect your thoroughness. If they don't, you are probably in the wrong place.

The American Medical Directors Association provides excellent questions to ask regarding problems with quality of care reported by nursing homes themselves. www.amda.com, click on *Consumer Corner.*

◄ *The inspection report, including any violations of requirements for quality of care, must be posted in plain view at every nursing home. If it is not, be suspicious. Ask why it isn't. If you haven't read it yet, now is the time.*

Check on whether residents are sitting idly in hallways, unattended, in the afternoon. Visit at meal times. Are staff involved with the residents? *How is the food?*

A nursing home administrator told me that families should read the admissions agreement carefully. Look at the fine print. What's in the "Not Responsible For" section? For instance, "Not responsible for the security of glasses and dentures." Discussing that section, alone, will provide valuable information about life in that facility.

The administrator also suggested keeping these questions in mind:

▶ Is the staff welcoming?

▶ Do they make you feel at home?

▶ Does the staff take ample time with you?

▶ Are they open and specific about how they have resolved complaints or other problems identified in the inspection report?

▶ How does the staff determine what room your parent would live in?

▶ Could *you* live in one of that nursing home's rooms, even for a couple of days?

Shouldn't the effort to find the best nursing home at least equal what we do when we look for our own new home?

If several places are still in the running, get a good night's sleep and go back. What place feels best to your parent? To you?

▸ *Federal law requires nursing homes to empower residents to remain in control of their lives as much as possible. Which place seems the most committed to this principle? Do staff act as though it is their place or their residents' home?*

Does your father have a strong preference? If he can no longer make an informed decision or look out for himself, staff quality and the ratio of staff to residents become especially significant.

Chapter 25

Now What?

Your father has moved to his new residence. You hope and pray things will go well in this unfamiliar world. There are various ways to influence the quality of his life right from the start.

Help Your Parent Adjust

There are arguments for and against limiting your time with your parent immediately after he has moved in. Limiting my time would not have worked for Leila. Rather than helping her adjust, it would have been upsetting and disorienting.

Just as the nursing home's plan of care for your father must be tailored to him, so should the approach to helping him adjust to his new life. How you manage the adjustment period depends on factors such as his personality, interests, medical condition, clarity of mental function and his preferences. Whether he is upset by this move will bear heavily on how you handle the first few days and weeks.

Work on establishing friendly relationships with nursing home staff. Help guide them on who your father is and how to provide him good care. But don't interfere with their work. They have many other residents to care for.

📋 *You have the right to be with your parent any time, day or night, if that is what he wishes.*

If Leila had gone to a nursing home, my "adjustment plan" would have included:

▶ Get a private room.

▶ Keep Leila connected to her friends.

▶ Introduce her to other residents.

▶ Watch our favorite sitcoms; laugh!

▶ Get out in the sunlight and watch the birds.

▶ If Leila could handle it, get out for drives, go to dinner.

Take the Promises Seriously

Federal law requires nursing homes to help each resident "attain and maintain" his or her highest level of well-being, physically, mentally and emotionally. Consequently, to qualify for federal and state funding, nursing homes make important "promises" it can be difficult to keep. These promises include:

If it is possible for a resident to get better, he will.

The health and strength of some residents should *improve* once they receive care they didn't have outside the facility. For instance, some people who enter the nursing home in wheelchairs should respond to treatment that gets them back on their feet. It also should mean that some of these residents will be able to leave for another kind of residence, such as assisted living, or even return to their homes.

This promise applies to every resident, not just those who enter a nursing home for short-term therapy covered by Medicare.

Residents' health, strength and mobility will not decline due to nursing home care.

State inspectors look for these kinds of indicators of poor care: weight loss after entering a nursing facility, skin sores that do not heal ("pressure sores"), the onset of incontinence, loss of the ability to walk, and decline in mental health. You should watch for these kinds of problems from the time your parent moves in. (See *Nursing Home Compare*. Click on: *Quality*.)

These promises should be your expectations and nursing home staff should understand that they are.

I interviewed a former nursing home Director of Nursing who is now a home healthcare manager. She provides an insider's perspective on what families should do—and not do—to work well with nursing home staff. Her comments run throughout the rest of this Part.

Become an Instant Partner in "Care Planning"

Nursing homes are required to develop a detailed plan for your parent's medical care and for every other aspect of daily life. They must involve your parent and you in creating this plan, and in changing it, to the extent that you wish to participate. Partnering with nursing home staff on the care plan, and keeping track of whether it is working, are among the most powerful ways to ensure your parent's well-being.

Each individual's plan should be tailored to her needs, not to what is easiest for staff. It should build on her strengths and not just focus on what she cannot do. A good plan would reflect her lifestyle preferences and interests. The ideal care plan for Leila would have included:

▸ A late breakfast in her room.

▸ A bath or shower in mid-morning. Because Leila was so frail, it was difficult for her to get going in the morning.

▸ Introductions to other residents with similar interests, for instance people who enjoyed crossword puzzles.

▸ Real-life physical therapy. For Leila to stay strong physically and emotionally she would have been assisted to walk to the dining room and outdoors to enjoy the sunshine. She would have used the wheelchair only when it was best for her.

▸ Life in the community. Going out to lunch or dinner a couple times a week would have been a priority. Friends and family would have helped.

The plan, of course, would be far more detailed.

Director of Nursing: *"Set measurable goals whenever you can. Then check on progress in reaching those goals. For instance: Your parent is to receive therapy in order to be self-sufficient when he eats.*

"Measurable goals might include: 'Drinks from glass without spilling by (date). Able to use knife to cut up meat by (date)'. Now and then check on where they are with measurements."

For detailed assistance with care planning go to www.nccnhr.com. Click on *Fact Sheets.* This is the web site for the National Citizens Coalition for Nursing Home Reform.

Chapter 26

Managing Life Day-to-Day

Control was one of the reasons I fought to keep Leila out of a nursing home. I didn't want to us to lose it. Friends would sometimes laugh at this perception of our home life. *We had control?* I had to juggle schedules constantly. Caregivers were coming and going and sometimes calling in sick. Life at times was chaotic. But it was *our* chaos. If the schedule was messed up, it was still our schedule and we would fix it.

Once you enter a nursing home it is no longer your mother's schedule. Or yours. It is theirs. The best nursing homes are trying to change. They work hard on individualizing daily life. Nevertheless, in even the best places it is often difficult to do. You need to help them. To succeed, you have to take back some control.

"As strong as she can" should remain your focus and it may be your *greatest challenge.* Your parent will need you and the strategies you learn in this guide at least as much as she did before she became a nursing home resident.

Stay in Charge of Your Parent's Medical Care

CB∞

Ben's mother, Gladys, had been doing well in her own apartment. Then she fell and hurt her back. After a short hospital stay, Gladys was discharged to a nursing home for rehabilitation. It soon appeared that she should remain there. Gladys was confused, weak and had a breathing problem that the nursing home physician believed was untreatable.

Ben asked me what I thought he should do. He told me, "I think I should get her out of there." I told him his instincts were on target and that his mother's disorientation might fade rapidly once she left. I suggested that he should have her medical problems and medications assessed by a physician skilled in geriatric medicine.

Ben took her to see his doctor on a Monday. The physician found that she had a respiratory infection and prescribed an antibiotic. He discontinued a medication that was probably contributing to her confusion. At his suggestion, Ben had his mother discharged from the nursing facility.

Gladys moved in with Ben's family temporarily. Her first request: "A big spaghetti dinner." By the weekend, Gladys' breathing problem had improved and she was strong enough to get around by herself. She was no longer confused.

Gladys moved back to her apartment. Within two months she was driving again. Her son's common sense and assertive advocacy, together with her new physician's skill and advice, had saved her life.

CB∞

A few tips

- If your parent has a doctor who provided him good care before he moved to the nursing home, go out of your way to help him continue to see this physician. Your parent's doctor has the right to immediate access to the nursing home to see him and his other patients.

- Most nursing home residents are under the care of doctors who work in those facilities. Sometimes they collaborate with the resident's regular doctor. Do not assume that facility physicians are trained in geriatric medicine.

- Help any new physician understand your parent's medical needs.

- Do not assume that a decline in your parent's physical or mental health is inevitable. Trust your instincts.

- Follow the same steps to protect your parent from errors and misdiagnoses as you would in the hospital.

- Watch for inappropriate use of prescription medications.

- Pay attention to your parent's mental health. Many nursing home residents experience depression shortly after moving in.

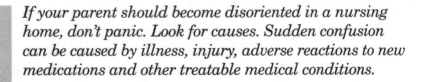

If your parent should become disoriented in a nursing home, don't panic. Look for causes. Sudden confusion can be caused by illness, injury, adverse reactions to new medications and other treatable medical conditions.

The nursing home environment, alone, can cause or worsen a resident's disorientation. See Chapter 2 for more on sudden confusion.

Make Individualize Your Daily Goal

You and your parent have helped staff develop a plan that matches your parent's needs and personality. It will take hard work and education of the staff to bring it to life.

The little things matter

ᘓᘔ

Rhonda helped her aunt adjust to life in a nursing home. "Many things she used a lot, such as her nail file, magazines, even her box of facial tissues, were kept too far from her bed. She could not reach them. Same thing when she sat in her chair. Her aides said she should just call them when she needed something.

My aunt was extremely frustrated. She felt she didn't have control of her life. I suggested to staff that they rearrange her room so she could get at these little things that meant so much to her. They did. It made a world of difference to her."

ᘔᘓ

"But Mom, everyone else likes it."

ᘓᘔ

I asked Mary Lou, a resident in an assisted living building, if she enjoyed the recreation activities. "They are fine. . .if you like bingo and Hearts." We both laughed. I knew Mary Lou preferred solitude, by far, over those options.

ᘔᘓ

Director of Nursing: "Assist staff to design and redesign your parent's day—for instance, his recreation activities. You can make sure your dad goes to group activities but he can end up sleeping there from boredom."

Watch out for early to bed and early to rise

Director of Nursing: *"To check on individualization, make surprise visits, early evening and in the morning. If your dad's plan calls for nine p.m. bedtime and he is in bed at seven, why is he in bed? Get him up again unless it is what he wanted."*

If this kind of deviation from the plan happens frequently, ask staff managers to get it back on track.

Make continuity of care a priority

In the Leila-and-Terry Years, some of our most difficult times were when we had to "break in" a new caregiver. I had to be sure Leila was comfortable with her and that she was trustworthy. I would have to work with the aide until she understood Leila's preferences and the best and safest ways to care for her. Many times I thought: "Might as well just do this myself." But I knew these training sessions would pay off if the new aide remained with us for a while.

In nursing homes, providing continuity of care—having the same aides assist individual residents daily—can be difficult. Tell staff how important this is to your parent's well-being. Help make continuity a reality. For instance, if your parent dislikes a capable new caregiver, try to improve their relationship.

Emphasize Teamwork and Try to Avoid Conflict

Be helpful, not pushy

Assist the aides to understand how best to provide care to your parent but don't act as though you are in charge or the only one who knows anything.

Director of Nursing: *"Don't disrupt staff routine or interfere with the aides and your parent getting to know each other. Help your parent understand that what the aide is trying to get him to do is in his best interest. You can help the aides set standards for what your parent will do, work on and participate in."*

Give the caregivers a hand

I asked the former Director of Nursing how aides might react to a family member who helped out with baths or meals now and then. She didn't hesitate. "That's a family member they would love!"

Remember who the "customer" is

Director of Nursing: *"Aides and other staff have trouble when what the family wants differs from the resident's wishes. You cannot demand that some activity occurs if your parent says no."*

Get to know the social workers

The job of nursing home social workers includes looking out for the well-being of residents and assisting family members to participate in nursing home life. A creative social worker can make valuable contributions to the quality of your parent's daily activities.

Use the reassessment process

CB80

Eileen's mother, Glenda, fell and hurt her ribs during her first week in a nursing home. Eileen was furious. She became angrier when she learned Glenda was being wheeled to the dining room and her physical therapy had been discontinued. Staff said it was because of the injury. Eileen knew this inactivity would weaken her mother rapidly.

Eileen told me she decided "not to cause a fuss." Instead, she and her mother met with nursing home staff to modify Glenda's care plan. Two aides would assist Glenda to walk to the dining room for each meal until her ribs healed. Staff would also design exercises for Glenda that would help her remain strong in spite of her injury.

CR80

Nursing home staff are required to meet for reassessment of residents' plans at least every three months. These meetings also can be called whenever a significant problem occurs or there is any other reason for major change. Be strategic in these meetings. Act as a team member. Focus on helping your parent communicate with staff about the problem.

Catch Problems Before They Become Nightmares

Keep all your senses active

Even brief visits can give you a good idea of how your mother's life is going. How does she look and act? Is she losing weight or energy? Does she have more trouble getting out of chairs? Does she have body odor that may indicate poor hygiene? In privacy ask her how things are going. With what aides does your mother seem to feel the most comfortable? Has she had any upsetting experiences with staff members?

Give your parent hands-on help

CB80

It was early in the Leila-and-Terry Years. A new home health aide, Roberta, had been giving Leila her baths for a few days. One evening, as I helped Leila get ready for bed, I noticed a red mark on her hip. It was a warning sign. Unless we made sure Leila changed positions more frequently, the red mark would become a painful sore.

The next day I reminded Roberta that Leila's skin was fragile and that we needed to be more watchful. She apologized and told me it would not happen again. It didn't.

CR℘

Pressure sores are also known as "bedsores" or "pressure ulcers." They are a common and serious problem for frail elders who cannot move around on their own or shift their weight when they are lying down or sitting. *If these sores become infected they can be deadly.*

Other common problems related to inadequate care

▶ Weight loss

▶ Loss of ability to care for oneself

▶ Loss of control of bowels or bladder

▶ Inadequately controlled pain

▶ Urinary tract infections

The Quality Measures on Nursing Home Compare (NHC) list the major care-related problems affecting nursing home residents and their families nationwide. These measures are organized by problems affecting long-term residents and those affecting short-term residents. Go to www.Medicare.gov, search for *Nursing Home Compare.*

Look, also, at the Nursing Home Awareness Campaign Alerts. Alerts relate to major prevention issues facing nursing homes, such as preventing malnutrition and dehydration. Click on *Resources.*

◧ *You also should be concerned about preventing accidents from falls.*

As in Leila's case, problems can result from mistakes by otherwise careful aides. For instance, when I told another of our homecare aides about

Leila's red mark, she said: "Terry, I am so sorry! I took it for granted that Roberta was looking for pressure sores." Of course, many problems also occur with the inevitable deterioration of a resident's medical condition. For instance, people in advanced stages of Alzheimer's disease often experience uncontrollable incontinence. Sometimes these problems can result from a pattern of neglect, which is a form of abuse. (See page 243.)

Director of Nursing: *"Things happen. We (nurses and aides) can make mistakes. If it is an uncommon incident, don't treat it as a terrible thing you need to complain about or sue about. Don't be accusatory; don't make it personal. Talk about the specific problem, what you are worried about. Never say: 'You are not doing your job.'"*

Be vigilant about nutrition and hydration

ೞ൏

Mary Lou takes her meals in a group dining room in her assisted living residence. The aides try to help the residents to eat well, but they have trouble finding the time. Sometimes the food is not appetizing. I recently took Mary Lou to lunch. I noticed she had lost weight. Mary Lou told me she hadn't had much of an appetite lately and ordered soup and crackers. "Maybe I will have a piece of fruit later in my room."

I ordered a large salad loaded with vegetables, chunks of cheese and egg slices and encouraged Mary Lou to try it. I had to describe the salad to her because of her poor vision. I guided Mary Lou through her lunch. "How about a tomato slice? And there is a slice of egg with your name on it next to the tomato." We topped off our lunch with raspberry sherbet and coffee. On our way back, Mary Lou said "Boy, I was hungrier than I thought I was."

ೞ൏

It can be especially difficult for nursing home staff to assist each resident at mealtime. Check frequently on what and how much your father is eating. Dehydration and malnutrition can occur rapidly in fragile elders. Ask staff about the warning signs. *As in hospitals, if your parent is not eating, ask the dietitian for help.*

You will do no greater favor to your parent, or to her caregivers, than dropping in at mealtime as often as you can. This is where a campaign can be invaluable. See the next chapter.

Read your parent's care records

Your parent has authority to grant you permanent access to her medical records and the staff's daily notes on her care. Reading these records is essential. For instance, they could indicate a problem, such as incontinence, that no one has reported to you.

You will find useful information on concerns other than health, such as problems related to your mother's recreation activities. Records review gives you a useful snapshot of what has been going on in your parent's daily life. If you have trouble deciphering the language, you will not be the first family member with that problem. Get help from the staff. Soon you will be an expert records reviewer.

Staff may not be aware of your right to this information. Much of it may be stored electronically. Don't let these bumps throw you. Your rights include the right to paper copies. Ask the social worker to help you.

Watch for Harmful Use of Restraints

Nursing homes have a history of inappropriate restraint of their residents, both chemically and physically.

A physical restraint is any device used to limit a person's ability to move or use a part of his body. Examples are safety bars on wheelchairs, ties on a resident's legs or arms, and mittens that prevent full use of a person's hands. A chemical restraint is the use of a drug not to treat a resident's medical symptoms but to control her behavior, to discipline her, or for the convenience of nursing home staff. These drugs are grouped as "psychoactive" medications. They are used to treat conditions such as anxiety, insomnia, depression, and manic and psychotic behavior.

▣ *Restraints must never be used for discipline or staff convenience.*

It violates federal law to use either restraint unless it is medically necessary and the resident or her legal representative approves it. However, staff may temporarily restrain a resident physically without prior approval or a physician's orders in emergency situations, for instance to keep a person from harming himself or others.

Nursing homes must use other methods to treat a resident's problems before resorting to restraints. For instance, where a person is at high risk for falls, the physician's care plan would emphasize improving the resident's strength and balance. If a restraint must be used, the nursing home must continue working to reduce or eliminate the need for it.

Staff sometimes mistakenly use physical restraints to improve resident safety. Often, however, the use of restraints *reduces* safety because residents become weaker and less mobile. Restraint use also leads to pressure sores and other medical problems including depression and incontinence.

I was privileged to sit in on a meeting of the behavior committee of a Wisconsin nursing home. The facility's residents have Alzheimer's disease and other types of dementia. The committee reviewed the use of medications prescribed to improve the mood or behavior of specific residents. I signed a confidentiality form and the staff did not use residents' names. The residents' problems included extreme agitation or anger, profound depression and sadness, and violent acts against staff or other residents.

In each case, staff members described the problem and discussed its likely causes. If it might be a medication, they reduced the dosage, eliminated it from the care plan or agreed to try another. They always looked for ways to resolve the problem before deciding to increase medication dosage or add a drug to the person's care plan. They looked for medical causes, such as a urinary-tract infection, or for an upsetting change in the resident's life, for instance, a new roommate.

Families of people with dementia should look for and expect this kind of careful use of chemical restraints.

Many nursing facilities are working to limit the use of restraints. Some have adopted "restraint free" practices. Some facilities are not as successful as others at changing their practices. Stay alert.

The California Department of Human Services has an excellent, consumer-friendly discussion on restraints at www.dhs.ca.gov, search for *Nursing home residents' rights.*

Limit the Number of Cooks

You will want a number of your parent's visitors to keep track of how she is doing. Do not have them raise concerns with staff unless there is an urgent problem. Keep that responsibility for yourself and perhaps one other family member or friend. Busy aides and nurses do not need, or appreciate, several visitors trying to direct resident care.

Remember, federal law prohibits staff from sharing anything about your parent's medical condition or treatments with anyone who is not authorized to receive this information. This includes family members.

Chapter 27

Build a World Within the Nursing Home World

The list of "what you should do" to ensure your parent's well-being in a nursing home is daunting. Investing a substantial amount of time at first may enable you to relax later. In most cases, however, you will need to remain at least as involved as you were before your parent entered nursing home life, especially when he no longer can look out for himself.

To hang in there over the long run and maintain your own health, be creative at getting others involved in helping you and nursing home staff bring the care plan to life. Work at building a campaign. A well-organized campaign can be a powerful way to make sure your parent gets good care and has a rich life. (See pages 62 and 139, for more on campaign-building.)

Even if staff do not like your parent they are likely to give him more attention when the behavior of family and friends says *"Something important is going on here. This is someone we care about. Get on board."*

An effective campaign

▶ makes clear to staff they will be held accountable every day for the quality of care they provide your parent.

235

▸ enriches your parent's daily life.

▸ lets staff know that you do not take their hard work for granted. Some staff members will become allies if you honor what they do for your parent.

Some essential steps for building a dynamic campaign within the nursing home world:

Get to Work on the Labels

When staff see your father as "Richard," rather than "the new patient in 152," the quality of his life is likely to improve. Decorate his living area with valued possessions. A few small pictures, such as photos of grandchildren, can have a large impact. Bring in scrapbooks of family life. Get him to talk about his work.

🔌 *Keep valuables locked up. Theft of personal belongings is not uncommon in some nursing homes.*

Enlist Your Parent's Community

Building a campaign in a nursing home is more complicated than it is in a hospital. It is a long-term challenge. You will need to involve more people. Scheduling visits will be more demanding, at least at first. It will take time to get organized.

Encourage visits by friends, neighbors, and other family members.

Residents' Rights include the right to visits by relatives at any time of day or night. Friends may visit at most times but the nursing home may put "reasonable restrictions" on these visits. For instance, it is reasonable to deny most friends the right to a 3 a.m. visit. However, if your parent has a close friend who can visit more often than you can, the nursing home may grant him 'round-the-clock visiting rights.

Expand your parent's social circle.

▶ Ask staff for ideas and contacts. Social workers may be especially helpful.

▶ Recruit volunteers. You may find people who will visit your parent by contacting schools, your parent's church, senior centers and community volunteer agencies. Ombudsmen agencies have volunteers in some communities who visit nursing homes. They may not make special visits to your parent but they can stop by when they are in her nursing home. They may have suggestions on how to find other volunteers.

▶ Get creative with homecare workers. Look for people you would have employed in your parent's home. If you find one or two who will spend short periods with your parent, employ them to do that. There are no rules against this but they should not take over the duties of nursing home aides. You might pay one of them to help you coordinate visits.

Your parent may be too ill or disoriented to appreciate visitors. She may prefer solitude. You still can promote the sense of *something important is happening here* by having people drop by, say hello and visit briefly with staff.

Develop Friendships with Staff

When a staff member becomes emotionally invested in helping your parent do well, you have a new ally and campaign member. Allies need not all be direct care staff. They could be maintenance or housekeeping workers, for instance.

Here are some additional tips for bringing staff on board.

Personalize individual staff members.

Learn the names of as many as you can. Don't tax your memory. Keep a notebook. Learn about something important in their lives. Use this information to connect to them. *"Hi, Carolyn. Is Becky over the flu and back to school yet?"*

Show respect to all staff.

◌ঙৎ◌

During a presentation to professionals who provide services to elders, I mentioned how much Leila and I valued the work of certified nursing assistants (CNAs). After the session, two women walked over to me. They were CNAs in a local nursing home. One of them said: "Thank you for recognizing us. That doesn't happen for CNAs very often."

◌ঙৎ◌

Most nursing home staff work under pressure much of the time. None have greater work demands than the aides who help residents with personal care needs such as bathing. Several have told me that some family members treat them "like servants." Don't do that. Treat hard-working aides as they deserve to be treated—like *gold*.

Director of Nursing: *"Avoid negative comments about staff in front of your parent. If you have a problem with the aide, work on fixing it in other ways."*

If you believe an aide or other staff member is not doing his job properly, give him the opportunity to change before raising the problem with a supervisor unless it is a serious situation. It is the respectful way to handle the problem and might be all you need to do. Who knows? That person ultimately might become an ally. And this way of handling the problem will build trust with other aides.

◘ *Be the family member nursing home staff want to help.*

Help Your Parent Develop Relationships with Other Residents

Nursing homes bring residents together for social and recreation activities. These activities can lead to new friendships. Leila disliked large groups. It would have been difficult for her to connect with others in group activities. Instead, I would have traveled with her through the nursing home to meet other residents and their family members.

There will be an additional benefit beyond new friendships when you take these social excursions. Many residents are extremely lonely. You will enrich others' lives as you enrich your parent's.

Build Alliances with Other Family Members

You will probably not be the only active family member in the nursing facility. Some adult children or spouses may have been visiting loved ones for years. Some might be excellent advisors on adjusting to nursing home life and also on resolving problems. If you develop trusting relationships, you might check on how each other's loved ones are doing when you are in the facility.

Federal law gives family members the authority to form Family Councils. If you can find time, get involved with this council. If there is no council, at some point you might have the energy to start one. State Ombudsman staff can help you. Being a constructive family leader can raise your status with nursing home staff. This can benefit your parent, as well as you. Also visit www.nccnh.com, click on *Family Involvement*.

▣ *Strategy should shape almost every action you take in the nursing home. If you meet angry family members who are alienating staff without cause, be careful about how you involve them in your life or your parent's.*

Assist the Residents to Increase Their Control

Federal law also gives residents the right to form Resident Councils. Your parent might wish to participate in council meetings. If there is no council, ask staff to help the residents organize one. To stay current on Resident Council success stories, contact the state Ombudsman and also do an Internet search for *Nursing home resident councils*.

The primary purpose of Resident and Family Councils is to empower residents and families to improve nursing home quality of life. Nursing facilities are required to provide these councils with private meeting space and with staff assistance. Administrators must respond to written requests from both councils, to act on grievances, and consider recommendations for improving everyday life.

The ideal relationship between staff and Family and Resident Councils is collaborative, not antagonistic. But council members should not hesitate to be assertive when they need to be.

Chapter 28

Handling Bad Situations. And Worse.

Bringing your parent's care plan to life and influencing the world around him will prevent many problems and enable you to correct most of those you cannot avoid. Be prepared, however, for situations where you will need to be an assertive advocate.

Bad things can happen even in the best places. When they do, it may seem that life has come apart. Your mother is living where she should be well cared for. Instead, her life is worse. You are already under stress. Having to go to battle for her can seem more than you can handle. People who are supposed to help you may seem more like members of the opposition.

Ask state Ombudsman staff to guide you through the steps you need to take to resolve these problems. Is there a nursing home advocacy citizens' group in your parents' state? Its members can be valuable allies.

Complain When Other Steps Fail

An aide frequently makes unkind remarks to your mother. Your father often smells of urine. You have tried, unsuccessfully, to work these problems out with the caregiver. It is time to take charge. Do not worry about "causing trouble." The nursing home has promised your parent a high quality of life.

✒ *Keep notes on every step you take to resolve the problem and on every conversation. You may need this information if you involve state agencies later on.*

Take the problem up one level

Tell the aide's supervisor about the problem. Do not be vague. Cite the dates and times when these problems occurred, if you can. Be clear that the situation is intolerable and must change immediately. Treat the supervisor as an ally, not the enemy.

Use the nursing home's grievance procedure with savvy helpers

If you cannot resolve the problem with the supervisor, try to work it out using the nursing home's grievance procedure, a formal process for reviewing residents' and family members' complaints.

Ask for advice and support from:

▶ Nursing home social workers

▶ Other residents' family members who have used the grievance procedure

▶ The nursing home Family Council

Ask state Ombudsman staff to intervene

If the grievance procedure does not work, call the Ombudsman's office. Ombudsman staff are empowered to investigate complaints and work with you and the nursing home to resolve the problem.

If there is a reason for keeping your complaint confidential, you may by-pass the complaint resolution steps and go directly to the Ombudsman staff. They will honor your confidentiality request. If several families have complaints, the Ombudsman is authorized to look for violations of residents' rights throughout the facility.

▣ *While you are working to resolve a complaint, don't leave your parent alone with an aide who refuses to, or is unable to, perform his duties properly.*

Act Immediately to Halt Abuse

Abuse refers to purposeful behavior which causes harm or significant risk of harm. It takes various forms, including physical, emotional, financial and sexual abuse. Abuse includes willfully neglecting basic medical or personal care needs, such as hygiene and nutrition. Stay alert for physical signs of abuse such as bruises or welts. If your mother acts uncharacteristically fearful or withdrawn, find out why immediately.

Elder abuse can occur in any living situation. In nursing homes, abuse is closely linked to staff stress, lack of training and to residents' abuse of their caregivers, for instance cursing at or striking them. Do not wait for a complaint process to work. Abuse is a crime. Go directly to the nursing home administrator for immediate intervention and call the police. Get the state Ombudsman involved immediately.

For detailed information on abuse in nursing homes, how to identify it and what to do about it, see the web page of the National Center on Elder Abuse, www.elderabusecenter.org.

Fight for Your Own Rights

The National Citizens' Coalition for Nursing Home Reform reports a national trend toward restricting families' involvement in residents' lives.

The NCCNHR policy director has been *"hearing reports of various kinds of intimidation and retaliation all over the country. . .When family members speak up about conditions in a home, they are sometimes banished, or their visits restricted or monitored."* (AARP Bulletin, The Battle of the Banned," November 2004.)

Federal law authorizes nursing homes to cut off contact between a resident and an abusive family member. There no doubt are times when families disrupt the work of staff and interfere even with the care of other residents. In these cases a nursing home may have grounds for limiting the visits of those family members.

However, any attempt to restrict visits by family members because they simply want improved care or safety for a loved one is illegal. Any effort to punish family members for organizing or participating in a Family Council is illegal. Report any violation of your rights to the Ombudsman and state survey agency.

Several initiatives in the United States are focused on "person-directed care" in nursing homes. These movements, essentially, are about making real the federal requirements for individualizing residents' lives. They also are pushing for "deinstitutionalizing" nursing home environments and making them more like home. These movements include the Greenhouse Project, the Eden Alternative and the Wellspring Model, which has its roots in Wisconsin.

Ideally, these movements will influence the quality of nursing home services and new construction across the United States. If a nursing home is your parent's only option, look for one that is committed to these ideals.

And never forget: Keep the Flame Burning wherever your parent lives.

A Closing Note to Daughters and Sons

C3⬙80

One evening in the last year of Leila's life, I was helping her walk from her easy chair to her bed. She stopped and, holding on to her walker, looked up at me and said, "Oh, kid, you will never have to say 'If only.'"

CR⬙80

You are working to help your parents live as well as they can in their later years, within the constraints of your own lives and your relationships with them. Please don't let guilt tarnish how you see yourselves if you cannot do "everything."

You may never hear your parents say: *"Oh, kid, you will never have to say 'If only.'"*

Let me say it for them.

Resource Appendix

The Resource Appendix will help you find additional information on topics discussed in this guide. These agencies and organizations are among the best resources I have found. Their web sites include links to many others that also can be invaluable.

Because much of the information you need changes frequently (health care and technology advances, for instance) this RA focuses on internet resources. It also includes toll-free numbers, where they are available, for the convenience of non-Internet users. Some agencies and organizations provide TTY and TDD services which enable people who are deaf, hard of hearing or speech-impaired to communicate directly with their staff.

Many government agencies and other organizations provide information related to the health and well-being of specific racial and ethnic groups. If the information you are looking for is not evident on the home page, try a web site search. For example: "Asian-Americans."

Other useful features

Many of these resource agencies and organizations provide on-line and print information for readers who:

▶ do not speak English

▶ have impaired vision

▶ prefer their information in audio form

Specialized assistance continues to expand. For instance, a web site that provided information in 2004 in English and Spanish might offer it in more languages in 2008. Keep checking each web site for improvements in consumer friendliness and outreach to diverse groups. Check to see if the organization offers publications on-line and in print format.

Most of my preferred sites are those of government agencies and not-for-profit organizations. However, some are operated by for-profit companies and include advertising. I have no connection to any of these businesses.

I refer readers frequently to the AARP web site. Although I am associated with this organization, it is as a volunteer on the Wisconsin Executive Council. The Council's focus is public policy. We have no role in promoting AARP products or commercial services.

⬛ *Where your need for information may be urgent, for instance when you are looking for assistance with medical problems, I include complete contact information in the chapter text for those resources. In other instances, the Resource Appendix will provide more detailed contact information than I include in the chapters, such as toll-free telephone numbers.*

⬛ *Always go to the Resource Appendix to look for more information if you do not get what you need from the resources provided in the chapters of this book.*

Key Resources

Some organizations and government agencies can guide you to national, state and local assistance on most topics discussed in this book. Their staff often have extensive knowledge of the communities they serve.

▶ Area Agencies on Aging: "AAAs" are designated by states to plan and coordinate services for older people within a specific geographic area (cities, counties, or multi-county districts). They can connect you to agencies responsible for managing local "aging services" and to every resource listed below.

To find the AAA office that serves your parents' area go to the web site of the National Association of Area Agencies on Aging: www.n4a.org. Click on *Links*.

You will also find these agencies, along with other kinds of assistance, on the Eldercare Locator web site: www.eldercare.gov. Click on *The Aging Network*. You can call the Eldercare Locator at 1-800-677-1116.

The AAA's in Wisconsin will be consolidating over the next couple of years. There will be fewer area offices. This may be the case in your parents' state, as well. Nevertheless, state AAA's will remain excellent information sources.

▶ *Tribal aging offices*

Aging services for Native Americans are coordinated through these offices. AAAs can provide the contact information.

▶ *Independent Living Centers (ILCs)*

ILCs also serve specific areas within each state and promote full participation in community life for people with disabilities. Their independent living staff members are experts on innovative ways to maintain elders' self-reliance, and are familiar with many government and local services. Staff of our local ILC were among our best sources of assistance.

The most efficient way to locate an ILC: Do an internet search for *Independent Living Centers + name of state* (using Google, for instance).

▶ *Aging and Disability Resource Centers (ADRCs)*

You will find ADRCs in most states. They provide "one-stop-shopping" for community services. To find a local ADRC, go to the federal Administration on Aging (AOA) web page: www.aoa.gov. Search for *ADRC*, then click on *ADRC map*. The AOA toll-free number is: 1-800-677-1116.

▶ *Senior Centers*

These typically are neighborhood or community centers that offer activities and services for older adults. Look in the Yellow Pages or contact an ADRC or AAA.

▶ *2-1-1 services*

Many communities are establishing information-and-referral services that are contacted by dialing 211. Go to: www.211.org.

Assistance with finding information on the Internet

You will find help with searching the Internet at your public library and also in many consumer-health libraries, whose staff will also help with researching medical problems. To find the nearest consumer-health library: www.medlineplus.gov. Click on *Other Resources,* then *Libraries.*

▣ *Many government agencies and other organizations redesign their web sites periodically. If you are unable to find certain information or publications by following my site navigation directions, try a web site search for that resource or kind of information. If you are looking for a specific publication, enclose its title in quotation marks. If that fails, it probably is no longer available.*

Health Care—Diagnosis, Treatment, Research and Patient/Family Support

◄ *These resources can assist you with diagnoses of medical problems and help you understand treatment options. Do not make decisions based on this information without first consulting a physician or another appropriate professional.*

Government agencies/other organizations with comprehensive health-related information

When I have limited time for finding information on almost any health-related topic, I begin with the National Institutes of Health web sites. The other sites listed in this section can often add important information. At www.medlineplus.gov you will find:

- ▶ information on over 700 diseases and other medical conditions, including Alzheimer's diseases and mental illness

- ▶ an extensive guide to prescription and nonprescription drugs.

- ▶ information on alternative health treatments, and on herbs and supplements

- ▶ tips on maintaining a healthful lifestye

- ▶ directories to hospitals and physicians, a medical encyclopedia and dictionary, updated news on health issues and thousands of clinical trials related to specific medical conditions.

MedlinePlus offers an excellent special feature: weekly news updates by email on many different health issues (for instance, mental health, senior health).

▶ www.nihseniorhealth.gov. This NIH web site is devoted solely to information on aging- related health issues. Its features include large print, easy-to-read information segments, and an audio function. Special buttons enlarge the text or turn on high contrast to assist those with poor vision.

▶ *National Health Information Center*

www.healthfinder.gov. Very consumer-friendly. "Just for You" takes you to information on special health concerns based on gender, age, race, ethnic origin, or role in helping others care for their health.

▶ *American Academy of Family Physicians*

www.familydoctor.org. Excellent, consumer-friendly home page, which includes links related to older adults. It includes links to useful consumer advice such as how to talk to your doctor or avoid medical errors. The "symptom checker" feature can help sort out the conditions which may underlie a medical problem.

▶ *Massachusetts Institute of Technology Agelab*

Do an Internet search for "agelab," click on *Resources*. Its health-related links take you to resources ranging from national institutes focused on specific diseases to university programs that inform consumers on important research findings.

▶ *Mayo Clinic*

www.mayoclinic.com. Includes assistance with thinking through treatment decisions and an interactive function that provides direct access to clinic specialists on a wide range of medical problems.

Organizations with Information and Assistance Focused on Specific Diseases and Other Medical Conditions

Most of the organizations listed below are non-profit associations or foundations focused on specific health and disability-related conditions. Most provide information and assistance that include:

▶ diagnosis, treatment and prevention

▶ managing these illnesses or impairments

▶ preventing falls and other injury-causing accidents

▶ the latest news on these medical problems and conditions

▶ research updates and information on ongoing clinical studies

▶ emotional support for patients, their families and their friends

▶ emotional support for caregivers, and resources to help them manage their responsibilities and their lives

▶ consumer assistance, such as how to locate medical specialists

▶ assistance with contacting state and community affiliate groups

▶ web site links to other organizations with related services and information

To find national associations and foundations not listed here, search for "national organizations" plus the specific disease or other medical condition.

Alcohol and Drug Abuse

▶ MedlinePlus has extensive information on the treatment of alcoholism and drug abuse, including links to many national organizations. www.medlineplus.gov.

▶ *National Clearinghouse for Alcohol and Drug Abuse Information*

www.ncadi.samhsa.gov, click on *Site map*. Toll free: 1-800-729-6686. TDDY: 1-800-487-4889. You get an all-in-one page which includes a list of the drugs addressed on this web site, and the many issues related to alcoholism and drug abuse, such as family violence, anger treatment and prevention. Some of its information is focused on specific audiences including older adults and ethnic/ racial groups. For access to information specialists 24 hours a day, including in crisis situations, click on *Clearinghouse Services*.

Alzheimer's disease

▶ *Alzheimer's Association*

www.alz.org. Includes links to Alzheimer's Association offices in each state. 24 hour toll-free helpline: 1-800-272-3900

▶ *Alzheimer's Disease Education and Referral Center—National Institutes of Health*

www.nia.nih.gov/alzheimers. Toll-free: 1-800-438-4380

Arthritis

▶ *Arthritis Foundation*

www.arthritis.org. Toll free: 1-800-283-7800

Bladder control and other urinary tract problems

▶ *National Kidney and Urologic Diseases Clearinghouse*

www.kidney.niddk.nih.gov. Toll-free: 1-800-891-5390

▶ *National Kidney Foundation*

www.kidney.org. Toll-free: 1-800-622-9010. Good information source on preventing and treating kidney disease and urinary tract infections. Click on *Patients* for an "A-Z" health guide.

Blindness and vision impairments

▶ *National Eye Institute*

www.nei.nih.gov. Toll-free: 1-800-222-2225 TTY: 1-800-222-4225

▶ *Association for Macular Disease*

www.macula.org. Information on preventing and treating one of the most common causes of blindness and visual impairments among older people.

▶ *American Foundation for the Blind*

www.afb.org. Toll-free: 1-800-232-5463 Includes a comprehensive list of special services for various kinds of assistance to elders with vision problems.

Cancer (all types)

▶ *National Cancer Institute (NCI)*

www.cancer.gov. Toll-free: 1-800-422-6237 TTY: 1-800-332-8615 Its written information for patients is comprehensive and easy to follow. The information specialists at the toll-free number are patient and helpful.

▶ *American Cancer Society (ACS)*

www.cancer.org. Toll-free: 1-800-227-2345 TTY: 1-866-228-4327 Offers toll-free 24-hour support from staff called Navigators who are located in each state. Cancer patients, family members, others concerned about friends with cancer may call their local

Navigator for help ranging from emotional support to assistance with managing medical treatment.

NCI and ACS have extensive information on chemotherapy: What it is, what to expect, and how to manage life before, during and after treatment.

>☐ *Most of these non-profit associations have strong state and local advocacy programs to raise awareness of these illnesses, increase funding for research and improve prevention. I know several women who find local advocacy on behalf of their cause to be a meaningful and therapeutic aspect of life as cancer survivors.*

Preventing injuries from falls

▶ *National Safety Council*

www.nsc.org. Toll-free: 1-800-621-7615 Essential information on falls prevention in and out of the home. Click on *Resources, Safety Issues*, then *Falls in the Home and Community*.

▶ *Centers for Disease Control and Prevention*

www.cdc.gov. Search *Falls Toolkit*. Toll-free: 1-800-311-3435

Deafness and hearing impairments

▶ *Alexander Graham Bell Association for the Deaf and Hard of Hearing*

www.agbell.org. TTY: 1-202-337-5221 Promotes the use of spoken language for children and adults with hearing loss.

▶ *National Association of the Deaf*

www.nad.org. TTY: 1-301-587-1789 Includes information on medical advances related to deafness and on available technology for improving the lives of deaf and hard of hearing persons.

▶ *American Association of the Deaf-Blind*

www.aadb.org. TTY: 1-301-495-4402 Assistance with improving the independence and participation in everyday life of people who are deaf and blind.

Dental Health

▶ *American Dental Association*

www.ada.org/public. Click on *Topics and Resources*. Includes an "A-Z" list of important topics, help with locating and communicating with a dentist, and tips on managing your oral health.

Diabetes

▶ *American Diabetes Association*

www.diabetes.org. Toll-free: 1-800-342-2383 Includes information on the role of exercise and diet in preventing and managing diabetes; also on the relationship between diabetes and heart disease and stroke.

Heart disease and stroke

▶ *American Heart Association*

www.americanheart.org. Toll-free: 1-800-242-8721

▶ *American Stroke Association*

www.strokeassociation.org. Toll-free: 1-888-478-7653 for general information, but their staff can connect stroke survivors and their families to a support line (Warmline).

▶ *National Institute of Neurological Disorders and Stroke*

www.nids.gov. Easy to use. Detailed information on all types of neurological disorders, current research and treatment, as well as lists of related organizations for each disorder.

Incontinence

▶ *National Association for Continence*

www.nafc.org. Toll-free: 1-800-252-3337

Lung disease and related problems

▶ *American Lung Association*

www.lungusa.org. General information toll-free: 1-800-586-4872

▶ *ALA Lung Helpline*

1-800-548-8252 This toll-free number connects you to a lung health professional.

Mental illness

The most efficient method for locating mental health information related to aging on these web sites is to search for *"Older adults."*

▶ *National Mental Health and Information Center (a federal government site)*

www.mentalhealth.samhsa.gov. Toll-free: 1-800-789-2647 TDD: 1-866-889-2647 Comprehensive information including links to many related organizations.

▶ *National Alliance for the Mentally Ill (NAMI)*

www.nami.org. Toll-free: 1-800-950-6264 One of the oldest mental health advocacy organizations. Provides information and support both to individuals with mental illness and to family members.

▶ *Depression and Bipolar Support Alliance (DBSA)*

www.dbsalliance.org. Toll-free: 1-800-826-3632 Crisis line: 1-800-273-8255 Has an extensive network of self-help support groups.

Osteoporosis

▶ *National Osteoporosis Foundation*

www.nof.org. Toll-free: 1-800-231-4222

Parkinson's disease

▶ *National Parkinson Foundation*

www.parkinson.org. Toll-free: 1-800- 327-4545

▶ *American Parkinson Association*

www.apdaparkinson.org. National Toll-free: 1-800-223-2732 West Coast: 1-800-908-2732

Wellness and nutrition

▶ *National Institutes of Health*

www.medlineplus.gov. Search for *Senior Nutrition*.

▶ *American Dietetic Association*

www.eatright.org. Toll-free: 1-800-877-0877 Includes help with finding nutrition specialists.

Information Specific to Minority Populations

▶ *American Public Health Association*

www.apha.org Click on *About Us*, then on *Public Heatlh Links*, then *Minority Health Issues*.

▶ *Indian Health Service*

www.ihs.gov. Information for American Indians and Alaska Natives. To learn whether there is an Indian Health Service office or healthcare clinic in your area, click on *Medical and Professional Programs*, then on *Area Offices*. For information on a specific health-related problem, you will find those links on the Medical and Professional Programs web page, as well.

▶ *National Indian Council on Aging*

www.nicoa.org Click on *Publications*

Managing Medications
(and making sure they are the right ones)

▶ *National Institutes of Health*

www.medlineplus.gov. Click on *Drugs and Supplements*. Information on hundreds of medications, including why they are prescribed, how they should be taken, and what side effects to watch out for.

▶ *AARP*

www.aarp.org. Click on *Health*, then *Prescription Drugs*, then *Using Meds Wisely*. Toll-free: 1-888-687-2277 Includes information on effective and safe prescription drugs, price comparisons, and a booklet on how to safely and effectively manage your medications.

▶ *American Society of Consultant Pharmacists*

www.ascp.com. Click on *For Public / Consumers*, then *Tips for Seniors*. Also *Seniors at Risk*, which includes an extensive list of medical problems that can be caused by prescription medication. Toll-free: 1-800-355-2727

▶ *National Center for Complementary and Alternative Medicine*

www.nccam.nih.gov. Toll-free: 1-888-644-6226 TTY: 1-886-464-3615 Detailed information on herbs and dietary supplements.

Low–Cost Prescription Drug Information

Prescription medication programs that help lower costs for those who meet eligibility requirements

▶ *National Council on Aging*

www.benefitscheckuprx.org

▶ *Partnership for Patient Assistance*

www.pparx.org. Toll-free: 1-888-477-2669 Alliance of pharmaceutical companies, healthcare providers and patient advocacy organizations that assists consumers to find inexpensive medications and free health care clinics. For people of all ages.

▶ *NeedyMeds*

www.needymeds.com. Non-profit organization focused on helping people who cannot afford medicine or healthcare costs. This information includes help for some people with specific diseases and other medical conditions. For people of all ages.

Guides For Health-Care Consumers

You will find assistance in the consumer-health libraries located in communities across the country, including help with accessing the web sites listed in this Resource Appendix. Many of these libraries are in community hospitals and medical clinics. Go to www.medlineplus.gov, click on *Other Resources*. You will usually find assistance at the reference desks of public libraries.

Finding the appropriate physician, surgeon or dentist

▶ www.medlineplus.gov. Search for *Directories*. Links to many organizations which provide help with locating the kind of medical professional you are looking for including dentists.

▶ *National Institute on Aging*

www.nia.nih.gov. Search for *Finding a doctor*. Toll-free: 1-800-222-2225 TTY: 1-800-222-4225 Also provides advice on how to talk with your physician to get the most out of your office visit.

▶ www.familydoctor.org. Under *Health Tools*, click on *Find a Doctor*.

▶ *HealthGrades*

www.healthgrades.com. Lists physicians by specialty throughout the United States. For a modest fee (under $15) you can purchase a customized report on a particular physician that includes information on medical training, whether or not the doctor is board certified in his or her area of specialization, and whether there has been disciplinary action taken against this doctor. Malpractice claims are not included.

▶ *American Dental Association*

www.ada.org. Under *Your Oral Health*, click on *Find an ADA Member Dentist* or on *Tips for Choosing a Dentist*. Helps locate dentists, by specialization. There are no quality indicators. Provides tips for finding the best dentist for your needs.

Asking the right questions; protecting your parents' safety

▶ *National Institute on Aging*

www.nia.nih.gov. Search for *Talking to a doctor*. Toll-free: 1-800-222-2225 TTY: 1-800-222-4225

▶ *Agency for Healthcare Research and Quality* (federal government agency)

www.ahrq.gov. Click on *Consumers and Patients*. Excellent guides ranging from asking physicians and surgeons the right questions to preventing medical errors, including in hospitals.

Finding the appropriate hospital

▶ *U.S. Department of Health and Human Services*

www.hospitalcompare.hhs.gov. Toll-free: 1-877-696-6775. An excellent no-cost report that will assist you to compare the quality of care provided by hospitals in your area. Provides quality performance information on specific kinds of care in each hospital, such as treatment for heart conditions, and compares the quality of care to the performance of other hospitals.

▶ *The Leapfrog Group*

www.leapfroggroup.org. Click on *For Consumers*. This Group consists of more than 170 corporations and other organizations that buy health care. Leapfrog gathers and reports information on hospital healthcare quality and patient safety efforts to help consumers make informed decisions about where to receive hospital care.

▶ *HealthGrades* (See above)

Guarding against safety problems in hospitals

Bacterial infections

▶ *Centers for Disease Control*

www.cdc.gov. Toll-free: 1-800-311-3435. Search for *2006 Infections in Hospitals*. You will find a 10-19-2006 release on infections in hospitals.

▶ *Yale University Hospital Elder Life Program*

Do an Internet search for *Yale Hospital Elder Life Program*.

Tips on avoiding confusion, talking to your doctor, and ensuring that you will be safe at home before you leave the hospital.

Sudden confusion

▶ *American Geriatrics Society*

www.healthinaging.org. Warning signs and common causes of a patient's sudden confusion (or delirium). Search for *delirium*. Toll-free: 1-800-563-4916

Medication errors

▶ *Institute on Medicine (IOM)*

www.iom.edu. Click on *Reports*, then *2006*, then *Preventing Medication Errors* report. Scroll down to *Fact Sheet: What You Can Do to Prevent Medication Errors*.

▶ *The Leapfrog Group*

www.leapfroggroup.org. Click on *For Consumers*. Their quality indicators for hospitals highlight major safety problems that hospitals are attempting to reduce.

Finding the appropriate home-health agency

www.medicare.gov. Toll-free: 1-800-633-4227 Click on *Compare Home Health Agencies in Your Area*. Provides information on the quality of services provided by every home health agency certified by Medicare.

▶ *National Association for Homecare and Hospice*

www.nahc.org

Finding help with paying for medical care

Financial assistance that may be available for people with specific medical problems. Search: www.medlineplus.gov for *Financial assistance*.

Background Checks On In-Home Paid Caregivers

▶ *State registries (listings) of certified nursing assistants*

Usually do not include independent aides, but that is changing in some states. You may not want to rely solely on a state registry. Sometimes these lists are not updated as frequently as they should be.

You can find your state registry easily by using an internet search engine. Search for *certified nurse assistant registry + name of state*. Some states may not have established this registry.

▶ *National Center for State Courts*

www.ncsconline.org. Provides links to state court web sites. Your state may provide information on whether the person you are considering has had judgments against him or her in any circuit court in your state.

▶ *Other assistance*

Many states provide public access to criminal records. To find this information check with a police department or search the internet for *criminal background checks + name of state*. The rules governing access to these records will vary across states.

On–Line Medical Records Storage Services

These services enable patients to store, update and share important medical information about themselves with any physician or emergency care center that participates in the service. You carry a card that emergency medical personnel can use if you are unable to communicate. The organizations offering this service will expand over the next few years. Do not use any such service unless you are certain that your records will be secure.

▶ *MEDEM*

www.medem.com. A no-cost service. Click on *For Patients* then *Create an I-Health record*. Toll-free: 1-877-926-3336

▶ *MedicAlert Foundation*

www.medicalert.org. 1-888-633-4298. Stores medical history, prescription drug lists, emergency contacts, and medical test reports.

Caregiving Assistance

These resources will assist you to manage the day-to-day aspects of helping your parents, including understanding yourself and coping with stress. Some will direct you to local caregiver support groups. Several of these organizations publish caregiver newsletters.

These sites also often have extensive information on the many community services available to help provide help and care to your parents.

▶ *National Institutes of Health*

www.medlineplus.gov. Search for *Caregivers*. An outstanding source of information and assistance ranging from preserving caregivers' physical and mental health to keeping up with the latest news related to caregiving. Provides links to many other helpful agencies and organizations. Excellent resource for people with dementia and those who are caring for them.

▶ *Administration on Aging*

National Family Caregiver Support Program. www.aoa.gov. Click on *Elders and Families*; then *Caregiver's Resource Room*, then on *Elders*. Toll-free: 1-800-677-1116

▶ *Alzheimer's Association*

www.alz.org. Toll-free helpline: 1-800-272-3900 TDD: 1-866-403-3073 Provides extensive information about Alzheimer's disease and how to help family members who have Alzheimer's. Offers a toll-free 24/7 helpline for those who need immediate information and assistance related to understanding Alzheimer's disease, caring for loved ones with Alzheimer's, and finding useful community resources.

Guides you to Alzheimer's Association local chapters in every state. Provides on-line interaction between people with dementia, caregivers and other groups, including health-care professionals. Your local Alzheimer's chapter will have up-to-date information about community support groups and provide telephone assistance.

▶ *Children of Aging Parents (CAPS)*

www.caps4caregivers.org. Toll-free: 1-800-227-7294 Non-profit organization begun in 1977 by family caregivers. In addition to educational materials, provides links to several states' support groups; also has on-line interactive caregiver support.

▶ *Elder Care Online*

www.ec-online.net. Provides education, information and support to caregivers, especially those who are caring for a loved one with Alzheimer's disease and other conditions that cause dementia.

▶ *Family Caregiver Alliance—National Center on Caregiving*

www.caregiver.org. Toll-free: 1-800-445-8106 Very consumer-friendly web site. Has an online support group. Offers online consultations for caregivers and news features for families, caregivers, professionals, policy makers, and the media. Information for those caring for loved ones with Alzheimer's disease.

▶ *National Family Caregivers Association*

www.nfcacares.org. Toll-free: 1-800-896-3650

▶ *The League of Experienced Family Caregivers (LEFC) University of Wisconsin-Milwaukee*

www.familycaregivers.uwm.edu. Click on *About LEFC*, then on *Useful Websites*. Also click on *Caregiver's Corner*.
Toll-free: 1-800-410-2586

Provides important information about caregiver resources, respite programs and support groups; it also gives family caregivers the opportunity to participate in a research project to improve supportive services to other caregivers. The League collaborates with an expanding network of state and local service providers nationwide to get information out to family caregivers about LEFC.

Family caregivers and service providers interested in this project: contact the League using its toll-free number or visit the League's web site.

Medicare, Medicare Advantage Plans and Medicaid

Understanding Original Medicare and Medicare Advantage plans

- ▶ *Centers for Medicare and Medicaid Services*

  www.medicare.gov. Helpline: 1-800-633-4227

- ▶ *Center for Medicare Advocacy*

  www.medicareadvocacy.org.

- ▶ *State Health Insurance Assistance Programs National Network*

  www.shiptalk.org.

Understanding the Medicare prescription drug program

National resources

- ▶ *Centers for Medicare and Medicaid Services*

  www.medicare.gov. Helpline: 1-800-633-4227 TTY: 1-877-486-2048

  www.aarp.org. Search for *Medicare Rx*. Toll-free: 1-888-687-2277

State resources

- ▶ *State AARP offices*

  www.aarp.org. Click on *AARP in your state*. Toll-free:
  1-888-687-2277

- ▶ *Area Agencies on Aging*

  Staff expertise includes finding assistance for members of
  American Indian tribes. (See Key Resources, page 248.)

Understanding Medicaid

The web site of the National Institutes of Health provides consumer-friendly information on Medicaid: www.medlineplus.gov. Search for *Medicaid*.

Area Agencies on Aging, Aging and Disability Resource Centers or Independent Living Centers guide you to reliable information and assistance related to Medicaid eligibility. (See Key Resources, page 248.)

Also ask these organizations for referrals to ethical attorneys well-versed in Medicaid law, and contact the state Disability Rights Agency. You can find your parents' state agency at the web site of the National Disability Rights Network: www.ndrn.org.

Abuse and Neglect

▶ *National Center on Elder Abuse*

www.elderabusecenter.org. Toll-free: 1-800-677-1116 Detailed information on how to identify abuse in any situation and on what to do about it.

In an emergency, call the local police department.

Legal and Financial Information

For "do it yourself" financial planning

▶ Try AARP's web site: www.aarp.org.

Click on *Money and Work*, then *Financial Planning and Retirement*. Toll-free: 1-800-687-2277

▶ The Medicare program also provides information and many resources to help with long-term financial planning: www.medicare.gov. Click on *Long-term care*. Toll-free: 1-800-633-4227

For assistance with financial planning

▶ www.cfp.net. Toll-free: 1-800-237-6275

The Certified Financial Planner Board of Standards, Inc. provides information about financial professionals and their areas of expertise. The Board's web site includes information on how to check on credentials and on the kinds of questions to ask of any potential adviser.

To learn whether actions have been taken against someone you may be considering, click on *Learn About Financial planning*, then *How to Choose a Planner*, then on *How to Check on Disciplinary History*.

▶ The American Bar Association and National Elder Law Foundation provide assistance with finding attorneys who specialize in estate planning and elder law. www.abanet.org. Toll-free: 1-800-285-2221. www.nelf.org

For help with deciding whether to purchase long-term care insurance

The National Association of Insurance Commissioners (NAIC) provides "A Shopper's Guide to Long-term Care Insurance." Contact the office of your state insurance commissioner for a copy of the NAIC guide and for other information. www.naic.org. Click on *NAIC states and jurisdictions*. Toll-free: 1-866-470-6242

Each state also has a State Health Insurance Assistance Program (SHIP) that provides Medicare beneficiaries with information and counseling on insurance questions related to healthcare and long-term care.

To find your state SHIP call the Medicare helpline: 1-800-633-4227 or go to www.shiptalk.org.

Information on reverse mortgages and on loans

The Center for Home Equity Conversion provides basic information on reverse mortgages and guidance on finding the kind that will work best for your parents: www.reverse.org.

For information on loans available to people with low incomes and people with disabilities use the Benefits Checkup tool provided by the National Council on Aging: www.benefitsheckup.org.

www.govbenefits.gov. A brief, anonymous benefits questionnaire will provide a list of programs for which you may be eligible.

For financial assistance that may be available for people with specific medical problems search www.medlineplus.gov for *Financial assistance.*

Fraud and Consumer Exploitation

▶ *AARP*

www.aarp.org. Search for *Financial fraud*

▶ *Federal Trade Commission*

www.ftc.gov. Click on *Consumer Protection*

Each web site provides extensive information on various kinds of fraud that elders and their families should watch out for including investment fraud, credit card fraud, identity theft, and travel scams. Check the FTC site for current consumer alerts.

Cost–Saving National and State Programs that Support Independent Living

▶ *Administration on Aging*

www.aoa.gov. Click on *Elders and Families,* then on *Services for Seniors.* Toll-free: 1-800-677-1116

▶ www.usa.gov. Toll-free: 1-800-333-4636 Federal government web site that you must visit. The introduction to its web page sums up what it offers: "Whatever you want or need from the U.S. government, it's here. . .You'll find a rich treasure of online information, services and resources." An excellent source for publications on money and taxes, consumer protection and more. Click on *Seniors*.

▶ *National Council on Aging*

www.benefitscheckup.org. Assists people age 55 and older to connect to government and private programs that can help them pay for healthcare, utility costs and other needs. On average there are 50-70 such programs in each state.

Benefits Checkup and usa.gov provide information on services available to residents of rural areas.

Managing Life Safely and Effectively

Preventing accidents

▶ *National Safety Council*

www.nsc.org Click on *Resources, Safety Issues*, then *Falls in the Home and Community*. Toll-free: 1-800-621-7615

▶ Centers for Disease Control and Prevention

www.cdc.gov. Search for *Falls Toolkit*. Toll-free: 1-800-232-4636 TTY: 1-888-232-6348

▶ *National Center for Supportive Housing and Home Modification*

www.homemods.org. Extensive information on home safety and modification and many links to organizations involved in home adaptation.

▶ *American Foundation for the Blind*

www.afb.org. Search for *A Checklist for Environmental Safety*. Toll-free: 1-800-232-5463

Managing daily life

▶ *National Institute on Disability and Rehabilitation Research*

www.abledata.com. Toll-free: 1-800-227-0216. TTY: 1-301-608-8912. Comprehensive information on assistive-technology products and where to find them. Its *Resources* link takes you to "all the internet resources known to us on a selected disability issue, all in one page."

▶ *National Center for Supportive Housing and Home Modification (See above.)*

▶ *AARP*

www.aarp.org. Search for *Universal Design*. Toll-free: 1-800-687-2277 Information on home modification.

www.disabilityinfo.gov. Toll-free: 1-800-333-4636 (Voice and TTY). Vast amount of information related to assisting frail elders and people with disabilities to manage their lives.

▶ *Centers for Medicare and Medicaid Services*

www.medicare.gov. Click on *Helpful Contacts*. Search for *Durable Medical Equipment*. Provides links to information on suppliers and on what equipment is covered by Medicare and/or Medicaid.

▶ *Independent Living Centers (ILCs)*

Serve specific areas within each state and promote full participation in community life for frail elders and people with disabilities, including people with hearing and vision problems. Their staff are experts on innovative ways to maintain self-reliance and are familiar with many government and local services.

The most efficient way to locate an ILC: Do an Internet search for *Independent Living Centers* + *name of state* (using Google, for instance).

Safe Driving

▶ American Automobile Association (AAA) Foundation for Traffic Safety

www.seniordrivers.org. To find "How to Help the Older Driver" and "Drivers 55 Plus: Test Your Own Performance," click on *Giving Up Keys*.

▶ AARP

www.aarp.org. Toll-free: 1-800-687-2277 Resources include an on-line safe driving assessment quiz. AARP provides safe driving classes in every state. Search for *Driver Safety*.

▶ The Hartford Insurance Company

www.thehartford.com/alzheimers. This takes you directly to "Alzheimer's, Dementia and Driving," a guide for families concerned with a parent's confusion and memory loss. It also is a must-read for other families as well.

Also see the Hartford's "Family Conversations with Older Drivers." www.thehartford.com/talkwitholderdrivers.

Options To Living at Home

▶ *AARP*

www.aarp.org. Toll-free: 1-888-687-2277. Click on *Family, Home, and Legal,* then on *Housing Choices*.

▶ *Administration on Aging*

www.aoa.gov. Click on *Elders and Families*, then on *Housing*. Toll-free: 1-800-677-1116

Also check with your parent's Key Resources for the housing choices that are available to them. (See the introduction to this Appendix.)

Finding the Right Nursing Home; Ensuring the Quality of Daily Life

Know the rights of nursing home residents

▸ *National Citizens' Coalition for Nursing Home Reform*

www.nccnhr.org Click on *Fact Sheets*, then *Residents' Rights*.

The Medicare Guide to Nursing Homes also describes these rights. (See below.)

Evaluate nursing home quality

▸ *Centers for Medicare and Medicaid Services*

www.medicare.gov. Search for *Nursing Home Checklist*. Toll-free: 1-800-633-4227. Also search for *Nursing Home Compare* which provides information about each nursing home, including

▸ The number of residents, whether it is Medicare and Medicaid certified, and the average number of hours aides spend with each resident as reported by the nursing facility.

▸ Whether state inspectors have found violations of federal or state requirements for resident care. Click on *Inspections*.

▸ Problems with quality of care reported by the nursing homes themselves. Click on *Quality*.

Also see: Medicare's Guide to Nursing Homes. Search for *Nursing Home Publications*.

► American Association of Homes and Services for the Aging

www.aahsa.org. Search for *Tour Nursing Homes.*

► *National Citizens' Coalition for Nursing Home Reform (NCCNHR)*

www.nccnhr.org. Click on *Fact Sheets,* then on *A Consumer Guide to Choosing A Nursing Home.*

► *The American Medical Directors Association*

Provides excellent questions to ask regarding problems with quality of care reported by nursing homes themselves. www.amda.com. Click on *Consumer Corner.* Toll-free: 1-800-876-2632

Contact two important state agencies

The state Long-Term Care Ombudsman and state survey agency are responsible for protecting the well-being of nursing home residents and helping residents and families resolve complaints. www.ltcombudsman.org. Click on *Ombudsman Locator.*

Ask Ombudsman staff how to contact the survey agency which licenses and inspects nursing homes.

Help your parent achieve the best possible quality of life

► *Centers for Medicare and Medicaid Services*

www.medicare.gov. Click on *Nursing Home Compare,* then *Quality.* Toll-free: 1-800-633-4227

The Quality Measures list the major care-related problems affecting nursing home residents and their families nationwide. These measures are organized by problems affecting both long-term and short-term residents.

Look, also, at the Nursing Home Awareness Campaign Alerts. Alerts relate to major prevention issues facing nursing homes, such as preventing malnutrition and dehydration. Search for *Nursing Home Awareness Campaign Alerts*.

For detailed assistance with care planning: www.nccnhr.org. Click on *Fact Sheets*.

Federal law gives residents the right to form Resident Councils. Your parent might wish to participate in Council meetings. To stay current on Resident Council success stories, contact the state Ombudsman and also do an Internet search for "nursing home resident councils."

Federal law also gives family members the authority to form Family Councils. Visit www.nccnhr.org. Click on *Family Involvement*.

Watch for improper use of restraints and for signs of abuse or neglect

The California Department of Human Services has an excellent, consumer-friendly discussion on restraints at www.dhs.ca.gov. Search for *Nursing home residents' rights*.

For detailed information on abuse in nursing homes, how to identify it and what to do about it, see the web page of the National Center on Elder Abuse: www.elderabusecenter.org. Toll-free: 1-800-677-1116

In an emergency, call the local police department.

Index

Notes~

Notes~

Notes~

Notes~

About the author ...

Terry Lynch is the Owner of Strategies for Independent Aging LLC. He has been advancing the independent living cause since 1977, when he served as assistant to the Director of the White House Conference on individuals with disabilities. He then managed a federal disability rights program and had a key role in developing what is now the National Disability Rights Network.

Prior to his involvement with the White House Conference, Terry participated in government initiatives to improve education opportunities for low-income children and remove barriers to school desegregation in Southern school districts

In 1980 Terry received a federal government award for initiating disability rights projects in minority communities. In 1985 the National Association of Protection and Advocacy Systems honored him with an award for his work in promoting the civil rights of people with disabilities.

Terry left Washington, D.C. in 1985 to establish his consulting and public speaking business in Racine, Wisconsin. He soon began living his work. Terry helped his mother remain at home for the next ten years, in spite of significant medical problems and a memory disorder that stole her ability to manage daily life.

Through this illuminating personal experience and his work with other families, Terry learned that we have more control over the quality of our lives as we age than we realize. His business is devoted to helping frail elders, people with disabilities, and their families maintain this control.

Terry is involved in state and national initiatives to develop "self-directed" in-home services. He also serves on the Racine County Commission on Aging and Board of the Aging and Disability Resource Center. He is a member of the Kenosha County Long-Term Care Workforce Alliance.

In 2006, Wisconsin Governor Jim Doyle appointed Terry to the state Board on Aging and Long-Term Care. He is a member of the Executive Council of AARP-Wisconsin and the Board of Care Wisconsin First.

His essay on making informed long-term care decisions is featured on the web site of the PBS documentary, "Almost Home."

Terry Lynch

To contact the author:

Terry Lynch
Strategies for Independent Aging LLC
P.O. Box 081075
Racine, Wisconsin 53408

Telephone: 262-634-8904
FAX 262- 833-0065
Email: TerryLynch@agingindependence.com

or

tplynch45@gmail.com

For additional information on Terry Lynch and his public speaking, training and consultation services, visit his web site at:

www.agingindependence.com

Beyond the Book . . .

Terry Lynch expands on his themes through presentations such as these:

Set It Then Get It: Maintaining Self-Reliance throughout the Retirement Years

Maybe It's Alzheimer's Disease — Maybe It's Not

"Old" Is Never an Acceptable Explanation

It's *Your* Life Too: Keys to Managing Family Caregiving Overload

Avoid the "Quantum Leap": Making Informed Decisions under Pressure

Doing Well After Fifty: Beware the Aging Myths

Preserve Your Self-Reliance — Conserve Your Assets

Alternatives to Nursing Homes: Tapping Community Resources

Remaining at Home in Our Later Years: When Is It "Too Risky"?

From Hospital Patient to "Nursing Home Resident"? Not So Fast!

Building a World within the Nursing Home World

Above and Beyond: A Son's Thanks to Direct Care Workers

Work Creatively with Families, Improve Your Outcomes

The Legal Center for People
with Disabilities and Older People

Colorado's Protection & Advocacy System

About the publisher ...

The Legal Center is a nonprofit organization protecting the human, civil and legal rights of people with disabilities and older people established in 1976. We provide direct legal representation, education, advocacy and legislative analysis to promote the independence, self-determination, empowerment and community participation of our clients.

The Legal Center promotes systemic change to sustain or improve the quality of life for children and adults with disabilities as well as older people. As Colorado's Protection and Advocacy System, The Legal Center has authority under federal law to gain access to facilities and records in order to investigate allegations of abuse and neglect. The organization also helps people obtain state and federally funded services, such as special education, mental health services, developmental disabilities services, and vocational rehabilitation.

Since 1988 The Legal Center has administered Colorado's State Long-Term Care Ombudsman Program and the Legal Assistance Developer Program under a contract with the Colorado Department of Human Services. The mission of the State Ombudsman Program is to:

▶ Preserve the independence, dignity, autonomy and freedom of choice of residents in long-term care facilities;

▶ Protect the health, safety, welfare, and rights of those residents;

▶ Prevent the abuse, neglect and exploitation of residents in long-term care facilities;

311

▸ Promote an environment where residents, family members, staff and others can work creatively and cooperatively; and

▸ Produce significant improvements in the delivery of long-term care to all citizens of the state.

The State Ombudsman trains and certifies a network of local ombudsmen who visit nursing homes and assisted living residences on a regular basis and respond to complaints from residents or their families.

The Legal Assistance Developer provides training and technical assistance to a network of attorneys around the state who offer free legal services to people over the age of 60.

Similar protection and advocacy organizations exist in every state and territory as part of a national disability rights network, and every state and territory has a long-term care ombudsman program and a legal assistance developer.

Since 2005, The Legal Center has published four books for national distribution, including the first and second editions of *The Everyday Guide to Special Education Law* by Randy Chapman, the bilingual Spanish-English version of this book titled *Guía de la Ley de Educación Especial*, and *"But I Don't Want Eldercare!"* by Terry Lynch.

The Legal Center for People
with Disabilities [LC] and Older People

Colorado's Protection & Advocacy System

Other books published by The Legal Center:

The Everyday Guide to Special Education Law
A Handbook for Parents, Teachers and Other Professionals
Second Edition

by Randy Chapman, Esq.

© 2008

Guía de la Ley de Educación Especial
Una Guía para Padres, Maestros y Otros Profesionales Académicos

Lic. Randy Chapman

Translated by Puentes Culturales
(This is the bilingual Spanish/English version of
The Everyday Guide to Special Education Law)

© 2007

To order additional copies of *"But I Don't Want Eldercare!"* or to contact
the publisher:

Web:

www.thelegalcenter.org
Email: publications@thelegalcenter.org
Phone: 1-800-288-1376 or (303) 722-0300
Fax: (303) 722-0720

Mail:

Publications
The Legal Center
455 Sherman Street, Suite 130
Denver, CO 80203

The Legal Center for People
with Disabilities ~~...~~ Older People

DATE DUE

Tell us what you think about this book . . .

▶ What information was most useful to you?

▶ Do you have a personal story you'd like to share?

▶ Is there something you wanted to know more about?

▶ Would you like to be added to our mailing list?

Email us at publications@thelegalcenter.org or call us at 1-800-288-1376.
If you'd like to be added to our mailing list, please indicate whether you
prefer email or surface mail.

Thank you for buying this book!